WIT AND WISDOM OF INDIA

WIT AND WISDOM OF INDIA

A Collection of Humorous Folk-tales of the Court and Country-side Current in India

PANDIT SHYAMA SHANKAR, M.A. (London)

Introduction by DR. SILA BASAK

PUBLICATIONS

KALPAZ PUBLICATIONS

DELHI-110052

Wit and Wisdom of India : A Collection of Humorous Folk-tales of the Court and Country-side Current in India

Rs.450

ISBN: 81-7835-675-9

Published in 2008 in India by
Kalpaz Publications
C-30, Satyawati Nagar,
Delhi-110052
E-mail: kalpaz@hotmail.com
Phone : 9212729499

Lasser Type Setting by: Rudra Computer Graphics, Delhi
Printed at : Singhal Print Media, Delhi

"CORK ME UP"

PREFACE

In rendering into English some of the quaint and comic stories current in India, I have had an immense difficulty in reproducing the original element of humour.

There are in India, as in every country, technicalities in jokes which are quite unintelligible to a foreigner unless he closely studies the particular racial and local habits and customs with which they are associated. This has compelled me to make slight modifications in the details of a few of the rural tales; and as the same story is told differently in different provinces I have adopted the version more comprehensible to the western reader.

The provinces from which I have mostly collected the tales are Rajputana, Central India and Bengal.

Our grand old men of India are in the habit of citing stories, such as in this book, to impress the moral of their advice or to caricature a weak character. Ancient Indian Logic furnished us with many popular maxims, based on short tales, which were cited to explain principles or expose fallacies—such as *Nripa-nápita-nyáya*, *Káka-táliya-nyáya*, *etc.*

I have tried to avoid the stories and fables of "Hitopodesha" and other Sanskrit folk-lore books, for they have been already translated by various authors.

To the best of my knowledge many of the tales in this book appear for the first time in English and some of them were never put into writing before.

One of the objects of studying the folk-lore of a country is to gain an insight into the primitive characteristics of the people.

PREFACE

In India we have the richest mine of ancient wisdom and an inexhaustible treasure of folk-lore. I have only collected a few tales to present to the west the lighter side of the country and by no means pretend to deal with the serious aspect of Indian Wisdom.

The predominance of stupid characters in the tales should not lead the readers to form a poor opinion of Indian intellect. The Aryans of India—inheritors of the world's most ancient civilization—are an intelligent people and can, with adequate culture, rank intellectually with any other nation.

So many ladies and gentlemen, representing England's best intellect, have—after a hearty laugh on reading the tales—assisted and encouraged me, that I am constrained to deny myself the pleasure of acknowledging my indebtedness to them by names in this preface, as their list would be too lengthy.

S. SHANKAR.

(JHALAWAR, RAJPUTANA, INDIA)

INTRODUCTION

Humour is defined in our dictionaries as a quality of the imagination which tends to excite mirth or laughter by giving ideas an incongruous and fantastic turn. That it possesses evolutionary value by relieving the struggle for life is proved by the fact that a sense of the ridiculous characterizes civilized man throughout the world. But humour is essentially a domestic product, reflecting the peculiar attitude towards external things which everyone, nay, every generation of the same race, adopts. Jokes which tickled ancient Normans fall flat on modern ears; many a comedy of the Restoration excites feelings of unfeigned disgust; "John Gilpin" which sent all England into fits of laughter, would have passed almost without notice had it appeared last month.

A quality so elusive seems to defy the translator and Pandit Shyama Shankar Sharma has undertaken a task of peculiar difficulty in endeavouring to familiarize Western readers with specimens of his native humorous folk-lore. Indeed, the gulf which yawns between Europe and Asia is wide enough to cause a suspicion that Indians are lacking in a sense of humour. Such is by no means the case. Stories gathered on Birbal, the jester and friend of Akbar, are household words throughout the Upper Provinces, and all Punjab; Rajputana has a Joe Miller in Lalbhujakkar who was the legendary fool with pretensions to wisdom; Bengalis have their Gopal Bhand and solace the "long long Indian Day" by retailing jokes unwittingly perpetrated by Raja Gabbuchand and Undhai Mandal.

Our author has passed through four Indian Universities;

he is versed in Sanskrit and the dialects of Northern India. He has travelled through the length and breadth of the country and has had thus an opportunity of collecting the folk-lore which survive in every rural village. His knowledge of our language and literature is equally extensive. He attended His Highness the Maharaj-Rana of Jhalawar during a prolonged European tour, and assisted him to record his impressions in "Travel Pictures", which was published in London in 1912. He is, therefore, a trustworthy guide for western students who desire to gain a deeper knowledge of Indian modes of thought. But I fully believe that his collection of tales will appeal to a wider circle of readers. They have a flavour of their own, and may be placed between the purely fanciful Fairy-tale and the Fable which conceals a moral. Our young folks will enter a new world, radiant with quaint imaginings, and their parents will discover an underlying vein of philosophic thought, and one proof the more that human nature does not vary greatly on the banks of the Ganges and the Thames.

FRANCIS H. SKRINE

CONTENTS

CONTENTS

CONTENTS

LIST OF ILLUSTRATIONS

Introduction

The book, as the title suggests, is a collection of humerous folk stories which at any time constitute an effective expression of experience at the ground level. Such stories have enriched Indian literature, as they have the literature of any other country. These may not be examples of refined art but the fact that these have survived through generations and are enjoyed even today can never be ignored in any discussion on literature as a whole. It therefore does go to the credit of Pandit Shyama Shankar that during his travels through the length and breadth of this country he never lost an opportunity to collect local specimens of folklore and translating these into English. Thereby he also performed the very important function of bringing the stories of one region to another in a language that remains the sole link in a multi-lingual nation. Translating is never an easy job, the flavour of the original often tends to get lost and it goes to Pandit Shyama Shankar's credit that he has ensured that any such loss is kept to the minimum. Going through the stories the reader may at times feel that he has read a slightly different version and he won't be mistaken. Folk stories often have different versions within the same region and naturally any compiler or translator has to pick the one that is more common than the rest. Certain words and expression are extremely difficult to translate and in this volume these have been retained in the original with appropriate notes to help the reader.

On the question of similarity, this is not be found only within the same region, similar themes can be seen in stories born in lands which are widely separated in geographical terms. The stories of Birbal and Gopal Bhand can be seen as examples of this. Both were court jesters, but the first in the court of Emperor Akbar and the other in that of Raja Krishnachandra in Bengal who lived in different times. Yet both Birbal and Gopal Bhand are seen making their royal patrons look silly and perhaps the only explanation is that in every age the commoner cherished the hope of getting the better of the ruler.

The collection has been named Wit and Wisdom of India. The wisdom brought to the reader is not that of a prophet or a sage but is that acquired by ordinary people through their day to day experience. And that wisdom of course had to be conveyed in a manner witty and humorous as otherwise listeners and readers would have lost interest - a story is so much better than a sermon. One such story is, *A Clever Broker Finds His Match* where the message clearly is, stay away from match-makers when arranging marrigaes. Similarly *Reborn As An Animal*, takes a mild jibe at the age old Hindu custom of feeding a whole lot of Brahmins as a part of the funeral rites.

Some of the stories of course are pure fun. The village idiot had everywhere been the butt of ridicule and India is no exception. From Bengal there is *Adventures of a Jamai* which speaks of the stupid Chuni Ram and his adventures at his in- laws' place, how he had totally misread his mother's advice to him and ended up not only majing an ass of himself but also losing his wife. Interestingly on his return home he found himself a much sought after man—"There was a great sensation in the village and people flocked to hear of Chuni Ram's advantures"—which went to show how people loved to hear tales of stupidity. And the stupid person need not be an ordinary villager, it is a king who is the central character in *Why Do Jackals Cry* and also in *Ullu Rai*. Every age has also seen learned men lacking knowledge in simple everyday matters and *A Learned Dunce* speaks of one such who is described by his wife at the end of the story as a "learned fool".

There are stories of a different genre as well. For instance *A Matter of Fancy (A True Ghost Story)*, shows how easy it is to be frightened of ghosts where none exists. The story is from an interior village in the present Bangladesh and is a clear indication that even at a time when belief in the supernatural was widespread there were people who could think rationally. And A *Question of Party Feeling* is very much contemporaneous with supporters of two opposing parties listening to only their leaders and shutting their ears to the others while an issue is being debated. Another storey, *A Question of Habit* says that any condition can become tolerable once one gets used to it. These are truly representative 'wit and wisdom' stories as also is *The Giant and the Pygmy*, and *A Little Knowledge Is a Dangeous Thing* in which Kanu Ram meets his death because he had tried to get along in life with the three English words he knew, 'Yes', 'No' and 'Very Well'. He uttered the first when asked by the English magistrate whether he had committed a murder, the second when asked whether he had anything to say for himself and the third when told he will have to die. This story must have evolved from a common desire to show off in the days when the British ruled India. Unfortunately though people invariably enjoyed the humour not many perhaps took in the wisdom concealed in such tales.

The folklore, by its very nature, cannot ignore social practices, particularly those adhered to because of tradition but are actually a curse. In India for ages there was the system of keeping married daughters at home and looking after the son-in-law as a guest for ever. One such story is *Hints For The Wise And Force For the Foolish* in which three such sons-in-law got the hints dropped by the exasperated in-laws and left home on their own and the fourth had to be driven out by force. And Female Gossip shows the kind of trouble that gossipy women can create for the innocent.

Of all places in this country, Lucknow was famous for its culture which laid almost undue emphasis on polite behaviour which at times led to ridiculous situations. Thus in *Politeness Carried to Excess*, two scions of the royal family insist that the other should be the first to get into a railway compartment and while this *apres vous* business was continuing, the train left the platform. Incidentally such was the culture also of Iran of old and gave birth to many satires on the subject.

The trouble that little knowledge of a language can create is also the subject of *An Unfortunate Resemblence*. An English nurse with only a smattering of Hindustani asks for a female donkey which can be milked, says *gadha* instead of *gadhi*, gets a male donkey and tells the man, "I want a ma'am gadha like myself". Could have been a real life story in those days when the English appointed nannies from their own country to look after their children as also did many Indian aristocrats.

Earlier I have spoken of the village idiot. Stories, however, also abound of the wise who are not exactly that. Thus wise man Lal Bhojakkar wept because the poor villagers did not know what a hog was and then laughed because he also had no idea what it was, something which he found extremely ridiculous.

Then there is *Undhai Mandal* (*Cork Me Up*) who was so sacred of his wisdom flowing out of them that he kept his ears, mouth and nostrils corked up for most part of the day except when he ate or was prevailed upon to give his opinion on very grave issues. As the story shows his advice very often, if not always, was something which the villagers could have done without but then there was nobody else who enjoyed his reputation. Rural society in India has always had its Undhai Mandals and Lal Bhojakkars. Or had them as long as ignorance was blises.

Life amidst the less than sensible can be at times very dangerous. This was rightly realized by the wise pundit (*A Fools' Paradise*) but not his stupid attendant with the result that he was about to be burnt alive when his master's ready wit saved him. Little wonder that Brahmin pundits have always been able to earn respect in societies dominated by Lal Bhojakkar, Undhai Mandal and their likes. Those who created such stories must also have been aware of this.

From humans to animals. The elephant is a beast not uncommon in this country but even then there are many stories about man's problems with it. Thus in *Is It A Chimney Or A Potato*, Bara Mia was at a loss as to what name to be given to the animal and ultimately hit upon 'egg of the earth' much to the delight of his equally ignorant neighbours. Included in the volume is also the one about a set of blind men feeling an elephant and failing to agree on what it was—Truth remaining elusive to the inwardly blind.

The elephant itself is an intelligent animal—even though fools are equated with it as in the expression hasti murkh which of course is used more to highlight the size of a man's stupidity—and so is the monkey. However, in *A Stupid Well Wisher* the ape is shown killing the same prince whom it had chosen to look after, while trying to whisk off a fly with a sword. Monkeys of course love to imitate and the poor animal was perhaps just trying to use the sword as it had seen its master do. After all the royal personage had been responsible for its training.

WIT AND WISDOM OF INDIA

CORK ME UP

I

IN a village where ignorance was bliss there lived a wise man, called Undhai Mandal. So wise was he that he would not let his wisdom flow out of him or have it wasted by wear and tear. With this in view he had his mouth, ears and nostrils tightly corked up, and would not open them except to eat and give his opinion when it was sought on very grave questions.

One day the whole village was set agog by a very unusual event. A boy, whose mother had given him some baked rice, took it in the palms of his joined hands, but had unfortunately put his arms round a pillar of the cottage in which he and his mother lived. So, when his hands were full, he could not separate them without dropping some rice, nor could he move away. He was in a fix, and the mother's cries roused the village. All hastened to the scene and took in the serious nature of the situation. Being at a loss to make out how the boy could be separated from the pillar, they all went to Undhai Mandal and made signs to him to take out his corks. Undhai Mandal would not allow himself to be uncorked too soon. So he was carried to the place and shown the plight the boy was in.

Undhai Mandal deemed the case worthy of his attention and granted the expense of a little of his wisdom. As soon as his mouth was opened, he broke out with :—

"I see the world would be all dark without me. You fools, don't you see the solution? Take off the roof and lift the boy over the top of the pillar. Quick now, cork me up again."

Undhai Mandal would in no circumstances, allow an extra amount of his genius to escape. So he took care to have himself corked up as soon as he had given utterance to his wise words.

The boy was safely lifted over the pillar and was free to move and use his arms. The mother was thankful to the wisest man for the clever way of getting her boy out of danger, though at the cost of her cottage-roof.

II

Soon after this event, Undhai Mandal was again called out from his retreat by the chief of the village to give his verdict in an important case. The chief's dear wife had dropped down senseless at the roar of thunder. The question was : "Who is to be punished for this ?"

Undhai Mandal was carried on the back of a bearer with due pomp ; and at his appearance the court rose up to do him honour. He was seated on a high stool, and the whole case had to be put before him without any loss of time as soon as his corks had been removed. No sooner had he heard the case than he pronounced the following judgment :—

" The potmaker made fire to bake pots ; that gave rise to smoke ; that gave rise to clouds ; the clouds gave forth thunder, and the thunder worked the mischief. So the cause of all this, the potmaker, should be hanged. Here is the verdict. Now quick, cork me up, cork me up ! "

The poor potmaker was seized and brought before the chief. The noose was awaiting him, but a difficulty arose which made Undhai Mandal undo his corks again.

" What's the matter ? " he asked. " Out with it, quick ! "

" Wisest of men," said the officers respectfully, " the potmaker is too thin. He is so skinny that the noose cannot tighten round his neck."

Undhai Mandal had the solution of all questions at his fingers' ends and he at once gave the order :—

" Go and search out the fattest person to be hanged in his stead. Somebody must be punished. Now, quick, cork me up, cork me up."

The Chief's brother-in-law proved to be the fattest person and he had to be hanged, for the order of the wisest of men had to be carried out to the letter.

Note.—According to the original version Undhai Mandal used to say :—" On the death of Undhai Mandal the earth will be enveloped in darkness. The moon of the sky will be eaten away by white ants."

LAL BHOJAKKAR

THERE lived in a village a man called Lal Bhojakkar, who was looked upon as the cleverest man under the sun by all his fellow-villagers. Anything that puzzled them was laid before Lal Bhojakkar and was at once solved.

Now, in the village of Lal Bhojakkar a hog was a thing unknown. So when one strolled in on a hot evening, it caused the wildest excitement. People rushed from all sides to see this wonderful animal, which took refuge in a pit. Some said it was a mole grown to that size, and others declared it was a reduced elephant, but none was sure. So here was a case for Lal Bhojakkar, and many ran for him and carried him to the spot. He was at once shown the animal which stood at bay in the pit, staring at the amazed crowd.

"Lal Bhojakkar, Lal Bhojakkar," shouted the people, "pray tell us what that animal is. None but you can tell us."

Lal Bhojakkar quietly took his seat on a slab of stone, became very grave and then began to shed tears. After he had wept for a while he dried his tears and suddenly burst into fits of laughter. This conduct of Lal Bhojakkar astonished the people more than the appearance of the hog in the village. They were wondering what could be the matter with their wisest man. At last one of them stepped forward and ventured to ask him the cause of his strange conduct.

"Excuse me, wise man," said he, "your weeping and laughing fill us with astonishment. Is it some inspiration that has come down upon you, or what? We would like to know before you say anything about the animal."

Lal Bhojakkar got up and in his wonted solemn voice spoke as follows:—

"Hear, my sons, I will explain. I wept because I felt sorry for you. What, I wondered, would become of you when I am no more? Just fancy your ignorance and helpless condition if you do not know such a common thing as is before us."

Here he paused a little, and the people shouted out—"But why did you laugh? You must have thought of something extraordinary."

"No," said Lal Bhojakkar quietly, "it made me laugh because it is so ridiculous that, to tell you the truth, I myself know nothing of the beastly thing you want to know about."

Note—In the version of the story current in Rajputana it is a crab that is said to have caused the excitement.

IS IT A CHIMNEY OR A POTATO?

MY next story is of the time when "John Company"* ruled over Bengal, and when the city of Calcutta was in its infancy. There were villages in Bengal in which potatoes were unknown, and there are still many where elephants are never seen. India had no railways then; so people who lived away from Calcutta died in ignorance of the sights of a great city. Yet the wonders of Calcutta were so much talked about that a man who had seen them was looked upon as a lucky person.

Now, at that time the Head-man of an out-of-the-way village, called Bará-Miá, took it into his head to go and see Calcutta. He thought himself too big a personage to be in the dark about the much-talked-of wonders of the town. So he set out with a few copper and silver coins tied at one end of his loincloth. After a few days' weary journey, he found himself in the suburb of the town. His heart gave a bound when he saw splendid mansions and parks, paved roads lined with shops, carriages and crowds rushing to and fro. But he

* East India Company.

could not help a cry of astonishment when he saw the chimney of a factory towering over other buildings high up into the sky.

"Hulla re Bhalla!" he cried out. "What in the name of goodness can that be?"

One of the townsfolk was standing by, and you know a townsman is always keen on making money any and every way. He at once spotted the raw villager and set about robbing him of some money.

"It costs a silver piece to know its name," said he.

The poor Bará Miá gave him a coin and was told that the thing he wondered at was called a *chimney*.

They had not gone far when they fell in with an elephant striding along, with a big bell tied to its neck, jingling at every move. Bará Miá could not suppress his wonder, and broke out into another question. His comrade charged a fee of another silver-piece, and told him that the huge moving thing was an elephant. Bará Miá felt puzzled to make out how the animal, having tails at both ends, could manage to eat (he fancied the trunk to be a tail). His guide—though he got a coin to answer this question—did not himself know how, an elephant ate, having never seen one eat; but he answered :—

"How clever of you to ask me. Few could answer you, but you can take it from me that it does not eat at all: it lives on air."

Presently Bará Mià's eyes were attracted by a basket of potatoes in one of the shops.

"I have never seen such big and irregular

eggs," he cried. "Can you tell me what animal lays such eggs ?"

The guide took another coin, and said, "They are the eggs of the earth—Gole Āloos."

Just then Bạrá Miá felt the knot of his *dhoti* containing his cash, and found it too much attentuated for any more questions, though he very much wished to know how the earth could lay eggs. Thinking that he had done Calcutta, having seen and learnt so much, he thanked his guide and marched back to his village.

On his return, the news of his having seen the town spread like wildfire among the villagers, who thronged in great numbers to interview the traveller and hear his account of Calcutta. Often before evening-circles he would recount the story of his eventful visit to the metropolis. "I have seen so many things" he would say "chimneys, elephants, and earth-eggs."

The people wondered and wondered, but could not guess what uncanny things they might be.

After the excitement had lulled a little, a gentleman came into the village, mounted on an elephant. It created a stir among the villagers, who had never seen such an animal. They all came out to have a look at it, but none could give its name. Then they thought of Bará Miá, for whom they all rushed, crying—"Bará Miá, Bará Miá, he has seen a town ! He is the man who can tell us what this animal is."

So Bará Miá was hurriedly summoned to a spot which the elephant was to pass.

Spying it at a distance he cried out in ecstasy :

"Did I not often tell you of this animal of which I saw many in Kalikata?* It never eats —fancy that!"

"BARÁ MIÁ WAS HURRIEDLY SUMMONED TO A SPOT WHICH THE ELEPHANT WAS TO PASS."

Just then the elephant broke a branch laden with mango and had a fine feed.

"Never mind," he went on, "it may eat when you fail to pay your guide."

* Calcutta.

"But the name, the name of the animal?" shouted the people.

Now poor Bará Miá had a bad memory and had clean forgotten the proper word. All the names he had learnt in the town got muddled in his brain. He fumbled about his stock of names, without getting at the right one.

"Its name, its name?" demanded the people.

Bará Miá muttered "Chimneys, earth-eggs: earth-eggs, chimneys." "It must be an earth-egg," he cried, and the people took up the word, and shouted out :—

"Earth-egg—earth-egg! Behold the egg of the earth, of which we have heard so often from Bará Miá."

THE BUFFALO OF THE KING OF DEATH

FADU MANDAL was a Devil incarnate. His whole life was spent in doing wicked deeds, and not one single pious act brightened up his dark career. He freely indulged in blackmailing, embezzling, cheating, chicanery, perjury, forgery and what not in order to "grab" money. The habit of annoying others for nothing was part and parcel of his character. He was never so pleased as when he had "done" somebody in some way. If any of his poor victims paid him back in his own coin, he would leave no stone unturned to wreak vengeance upon him. Yet so clever was he that he always managed to evade the King's justice by got-up evidence to prove that his acts were within the law.

When Fadu Mandal had become old, he suddenly remembered that his life was drawing to a close, and that he must do something for the hereafter. One day he found an old cow of his taken ill, and knowing that she would soon die, he sent for a good Brahman. When the Brahman arrived, he said to him:—

"Look here, O holy Brahman, there is no act so pious as the giving of a cow to a Brahman like you. And as I have to provide for a good hereafter I must do this meritorious act. So please accept the gift of a cow and bless me."

Saying this he gave the Brahman the old dying cow. The Brahman had a look at her and said :—

"Please excuse me, Fadu Mandal, I cannot accept your gift. The cow will soon expire and it would be cruel to take her out of the shed now."

But Fadu Mandal was bent upon doing the pious act, and nothing would make him change his mind. He insisted on the acceptance and accompanied his words with threats. Seeing the Brahman was still unwilling to move away with the cow, he raised his club and said with terrific menace :—

"I am resolved to do this pious deed and you have got to take the cow away. If you don't comply immediately, I will kill you with one stroke of this club."

The Brahman's heart sank within him and he had no other alternative but to take the cow and the risk, if he prized his life. He made the cow follow him for some distance, and in spite of all his care she fell dead before he could arrive home. The poor Brahman was hard put to, as he had not only to pay for the removal of the carcass, but also for a very costly penance in order to absolve himself from the sin* of having a cow dead out-of-doors.

Soon after this Fadu Mandal fell seriously ill. He was on his death-bed, when his sons sat round him and one of them said gently, still fearing to offend the dire old villain :—

* *Gau-hatyá pátaka.*

"Father, you know we have no money to pay the expenses of your funeral ceremonies. Will you tell us, before it is too late, where your secret treasure is?"

"No need for you to bother about my funeral," answered the father. "All my ill-gotten money has been ill-spent. My last penny has been swallowed by the costs of litigation. I am leaving behind nothing but you yourselves with the wits you have inherited from me. To aid your wits in order to find a treasury, let me give you my last advice:—Don't let anybody know that I am dying. As soon as I am dead, make a wound in my body and at the dead of night place it at the top of a bamboo-pole which you shall set up in the middle of a public road. Tell me what you will say when an inquiry is held about my death?"

"We shall say," replied one of the sons, "that some of your enemies have murdered you."

"That's like a good boy—a worthy son of mine," rejoined Fadu Mandal. "You must start your mourning when you get the news and say to the police officers that I had been summoned by the Zemindar* (land-lord) in the evening and that you know nothing beyond the fact that I went to see him. Now, everybody knows that the Zemindar and I are at daggers drawn in these days. About my funeral, you need not trouble in the least. I shall take care of myself."

* A *zemindar* is something like a lord of a manor or a squire. *Land-lord*, used to translate the word, should be taken in its literal sense and not in the sense of "the owner of an inn, etc."

The sons noted the instructions, and when Fadu Mandal was dead they took his body, under cover of night, to some public place and set it at the top of a bamboo-pole. No sooner had they left than the watchman of the village came round on his beat, and he was taken aback by the apparition of a ghostly figure perched on the top of a long bamboo-pole standing in the middle of the public road. He raised an alarm which roused the whole village. Crowds of the villagers streamed in and stood at a respectable distance from the spectacle. The police officer was sent for, and he arrived with a troop of armed men. They closed around the supposed ghost and commanded it to speak. But as it neither stirred nor spoke, the people began to throw missiles at it. Bang down came the lifeless body of Fadu Mandal, being hit by one of them. This put the crowd to flight, but seeing that they were not pursued by an evil spirit, they took heart and rallied again.

Then, with a few lighted torches, some of them summoned up courage to approach the object that had frightened them.

Discovering that the motionless body of a man was lying on the ground near the bamboo-pole, they had the pluck to draw closer and examine it. To their amazement they found that the supposed ghost was none other than the dead body of Fadu Mandal. The character of the sensation immediately changed and the keenest anxiety was felt by everybody to know how the Mandal met with his death and why his body was disposed of in such an outrageous way.

The police were extremely puzzled by this mysterious affair. They started investigations at once; and the Mandal's sons played to perfection the rôle already decided upon. Naturally the suspicion of the officers fell upon the Zemindar and he was placed under arrest.

The poor Zemindar was really distressed. He said to himself: "This devil of a man tormented me all his life and even at his death he has involved me in serious trouble." He instructed his agent to go to the sons of Fadu Mandal and to induce them to withdraw the statement that implicated him, by offering them a very large sum of money. The agent arranged matters as desired by the Zemindar. Thus Fadu Mandal left his sons well provided for, though he died penniless.

We now pass on to the sequel of Fadu Mandal's ill-spent life. As soon as he had died, his spirit-body* was brought for trial before *Yama*, the King of Death. The strict court of Yama keeps a faithful record of men's actions and passes awards according to their merits with unerring justice. The clerk of the court, Chandra Gupta, reviewed the record of Fadu Mandal's life and reported that there was not a single good act in his whole career on earth.

Yama addressing the spirit of Fadu Mandal said:—

"Thou wretched being, great was thy opportunity to do good works. But thou hast abused

* Ethereal double.

it. Human life is the highest life on earth hardly attainable by beings. That life thou hadst; but instead of availing thyself of the thousand and one chances to elevate thy soul, thou hast debased it by an unbroken series of bad works. Woe be to the man that fails to do even a single good work! I cannot give thy soul an upward course nor the even course of rebirth. Hell is the only place thou art fit for and I condemn thee to that." Thus Yama pronounced judgment, dooming the bad man's soul to the worst tortures of hell. Before he could be removed from the court, the spiritual Fadu Mandal cried out:—

"Is this the court of the ever just Yama, before which I stand?"

"What dost thou mean?" asked Yama.

"Only this, that your record is wrong or your clerk is blind," answered Fadu.

Yama: "It is impossible. Chandra Gupta has been working under me since the beginning of the last creation, and he has *never* made a mistake."

Fadu: "How then could my pious act go unmentioned?"

Chandra Gupta: "Pious act! You haven't one to boast of."

Fadu: "Please go through the record with your eyes open. It will never do for a responsible clerk like you to be drowsy."

Chandra Gupta: "My dear spirit of a man, I have examined the roll of your life as carefully as I could, and find nothing in the nature of a pious deed. Would you yourself mention the act you mean ? "

Fadu : " Why, what of my gift of a cow to a Brahman ? "

Chandra Gupta : " Ah ! You mean that ? But it was more sinful than pious. You simply forced a Brahman to take a dying cow, which cost him lots of trouble and money."

Fadu : " But then, I am going to suffer for the sinful part of the act. I must at least be entitled to some reward for the meritorious part of it."

Yama : " All right, let me decide it straight off. As a reward thou shalt have thy wish for one hour. Now it rests with thee to take the reward or punishment first."

Fadu : " I will have the reward first."

Yama : " Then name thy wish. I will grant it."

Fadu : " I want to have a ride on your buffalo which is the terror of the three worlds.* But you must command him to obey me as long as I am on his back."

Yama : " Thy wish is granted. But take care, he is the fiercest animal in heaven. It is only I that ride on him and never has anybody else dared tackle him."

Saying this, he commanded his buffalo to allow the spirit of Fadu Mandal to ride him, and to obey him as long as he was on his back.

In an instant Fadu Mandal mounted the buffalo and asked :—

* Heaven, Earth, and the World below the Earth.

"Buffalo, buffalo, whose orders do you obey?"

"Whosoever is on my back," replied the animal, "commands me."

"Then attack Yama-Ráj and pierce him with your horns," ordered Fadu.

No sooner had these words been said than the buffalo made for Yama with bent head waving the fierce-looking sharp horns, that were dreaded by all beings in heaven.

Yama lost his wits at this sudden onset upon him. Through confusion he upset his high seat and turned a somersault over it. Springing to his feet he began to run, followed by Fadu Mandal on the buffalo's back. Yama ran and ran till he came to Brahmá, the creating God, who was in a state of trance. No sooner had he been aroused by Yama's piteous cries, "Brahmá, Brahmá, save me," than he saw the dreadful buffalo rushing forward under the valiant order "Gore them both!"

Poor Brahmá had never been used to an attack like this. So he got up and took to flight. Both ran and ran and came to Shiva, the destroying god. Shiva too was immersed in contemplation, which was rudely shaken by the arrival of Yama and Brahmá, crying for help and being hotly pursued by the buffalo with Fadu Mandal on his back. Hardly had Shiva opened his eyes when he saw the fearful buffalo dashing towards him, being ordered by its rider—"Pierce all the three." Forgetful of his powers Shiva fled like a child. The three fugitives made towards Vishnu, the protecting god, crying all the while :—

"Save! O save us, Vishnu! Thou alone canst save us from the dreadful buffalo!"

From a distance Vishnu could perceive the miserable plight in which the three deities were. With a smile on his face he took up his shining weapon, *Chakra* (disk)—the mere sight of which was enough for Fadu Mandal to check the buffalo's mad career. Panting and fuming came the trio, still crying: "Save, O save us, Vishnu!"

"Will you please calm yourselves?" said Vishnu.

"There, there, look at the buffalo. He is coming upon us. Save, O save!" cried the three gods.

"I see him. He has stopped. Now will you tell me, Shiva, what it all means?"

"I don't know," said Shiva, "Brahmá knows."

"I don't know," said Brahmá, "Yama knows."

Now Yama, who had had the longest run, was simply gasping for breath. It was some time before he could regain his speech. Then he recounted the whole story, whereupon Vishnu commanded Fadu Mandal to alight from the buffalo, and asked Yama to take charge of him and punish him adequately. On hearing this Fadu Mandal cried out :—

"Protector of the world, is this a command which savours of protection? Need I, the humblest of the humble, teach thee thy duty?"

"What do you mean?" asked Vishnu.

"God of Gods, dost thou not remember thy own assurance that one who comes to thee can be touched by no power on earth or heaven? Is my humble self, who is now blessed by the sight of the Trinity, present before me, to be dragged away from here and judged by the ordinary court of Yama-Ráj?"

"Yama," said Vishnu. "He is right. You have no right to claim him now. He is beyond your jurisdiction. One who has out-witted you deserves special favour, which I grant him by allowing him to remain in this part of our heaven."

Yama obeyed and departed with the other gods and the buffalo. Fadu Mandal stayed to enjoy the part of heaven, called *Vishnu-loka.*

REBORN AS AN ANIMAL

ANCESTRAL worship is common among a large number of Indian people. Many pious Hindus daily remember their ancestors reverently and perform rites in honour of them. It is customary for them to feed some Brahmans yearly on the occasion of a ceremony called *Shráddha*. Although it it strictly enjoined by the Hindu sacred books that only one or two very worthy Brahmans should be entertained at *Shráddhas*, the modern practice is to feast a great many, worthy or unworthy. The popular belief is that the spiritual bodies of the ancestors get nourishment from the food eaten by the Brahmans at the *Shráddhas*.*

Now, there was a poor man who at his father's *Shráddha* invited hundreds of Brahmans. People wondered how he could have the wherewithal to buy materials in order to prepare food enough for so many persons. At the appointed hour on the fixed day all the invited Brahmans assembled in the compound of his house. But everyone was struck by the absence of anything indicating a feast. There was neither the bustle

* This belief is opposed to the philosophical doctrines of the Brahman sages, who recommend *Shráddhas* only as an honour to the ancestors and worthy Brahmans. The most festive *Shráddha* is performed within a fortnight of the funeral.

nor the noise characterising a *Shráddha* banquet. For an adequate preparation there ought to have been a huge canopy, at least ten ovens, many colossal utensils, an army of cooks and a large number of waiters who were to run to and fro arranging seats and plates, made of leaves, and keeping in order the different courses ready to be served. All these were conspicuous by their absence.

The guests did not know whether to stay or to go away, for there was nobody whom they could ask for an explanation. At last the host came out of his house quietly and cried out :—

"Do not wonder, O Brahmans. I have kept everything ready for you. You need only walk to the green at the back of the house and stand round the haystack."

The Brahmans did as he directed, being none the less amazed at the singular method of their host in giving a banquet. Many began to think that he was going to give a sumptuous feast through magic. They were expecting the dainties of a magical dinner, when their host, addressing them, said :

"Do not hate me, O Brahmans, as the son of a man who has been reborn as an animal. None can undo the effect of his *Karma* (action) in this life, and my father cannot claim an exception to this law. He appeared in a dream before me and said that he had done nothing but stupid acts in his life, and as a consequence he became a donkey after death. Bread, rice, vegetables, milk, cream, pudding, sweets and cakes are no good to a donkey. So I am not going to feed you on them. I offer you hay and grass and you must eat as much as you can, so that my father may not want any food throughout the year to come. With this, O Brahmans, I request you to help yourselves to the hay before you and the green grass in the field, and you may fall to eating at once. When you have had your fill, please bless my father and me, his worthy son."

Saying this he walked away, leaving his starving guests to utter "blessings" without even accepting his proffered food. Then they dispersed wishing the worthy son success in following in the footsteps of the worthy father.

A RAJA'S DREAM

A RAJA once dreamt of his father appearing on horse-back. He called his wise priests to explain the meaning of the dream. The priests, after consulting occult books, said :—

" Raja, the dream means that your father, who is in heaven, is not enjoying peace of mind without his old pet horses. You should therefore give away to Brahmans the horses that were his favourites. This pious act will have the effect of passing to him the *doubles* of the horses he wants to ride."

Now, the pet horses of the late Raja were the pick of the whole lot in the Raja's stable, so he was very sorry to part with them. But he had to do it in obedience to the priests' wishes and to make it appear that he was not lacking in reverence towards the spirit of his father.

The Brahman priests were very glad to have the best horses of the realm. But the Raja was feeling the loss very much. One day his court jester, seeing him sad, asked the reason. The Raja said :—

" Look here, I was very fond of the dear old horses I have given away to the Brahmans, and I miss them so much when I go round the stable ! "

The Jester said: "Your Highness, may I suggest some means of getting the horses back? It is quite clear that the priests played a trick to possess them. Cannot your Highness play a counter-trick?"

"What is that?" asked the Raja.

"Why," replied the jester, "call the priests early to-morrow morning and say: 'I have dreamt of my father. His body is wounded by a fall from his horse, and it requires searing. He commanded me to have the bodies of the Brahmans cauterized, so that the effect of the treatment may pass on to him.'"

"What a grand idea! I must do as you tell me," said the Raja.

The next morning before the sun had risen the Raja summoned all the Brahman priests and exclaimed: "Priests, I have had a shocking dream! My father had a nasty fall from one of the horses I sent to him through you. His body is scratched all over and he is writhing with pain. Nothing but cauterization will give him relief, and he commands me to operate on you, so that the effect may pass on to him. Therefore prepare yourselves, I am calling the physician to sear your bodies with hot irons. My father is suffering great pain and I must send him relief at once. This pious act cannot be delayed."

On hearing this, the Brahmans were very much upset. Many began to tremble with fear. But the head-priest was a clever man, and spoke thus to the Raja:—

"Your Highness, the dream has a deeper

meaning. Give us a little time to consult our mystic books, and I am sure we shall be able to explain it in a way satisfactory to you."

"All right," said the King, "but you must not be long. I shall have no ease at heart until relief is transmitted to my revered father."

"We shall not be many minutes," said the Brahman, who, having retired with his fellow-priests for a consultation, addressed them thus:

"Don't you scent something behind this story of a dream? None but the wily jester has fabricated it for the Raja to defeat our object of retaining possession of the horses. So, if you want to avoid the pain of being seared, return the horses straightway. Nothing else will satisfy the Raja and I can think of no other dodge to meet his."

The Brahman priests would do anything to save their skin and readily agreed to the proposal of returning the horses.

Then they went to the Raja and the head-priest explained the dream in the following words:—

"Your Highness, the dream does not mean what you think. It simply indicates that our Raja in heaven is tired of the horses and wants to get rid of them. So we had better return the horses."

The Raja wanted nothing more and expressed his satisfaction at the explanation, and in about an hour's time all the horses were back in his stable to his great delight.

"AN EMPTY HONOUR FOR A STARVING MAN"

THERE lived in a village near Delhi, a poor Brahman Pandit, who was a very great scholar and a poet of the highest order; but his merits were not widely known and he lived contentedly among his illiterate neighbours.

One year the crops of the village failed and all the villagers were reduced to penury. With them the Pandit's family also suffered. His wife could not make two ends meet anyhow. Stung by abject poverty she said to her husband:

"We are penniless. Every bit of our little all has been pawned. There is not a single morsel left to eat. Sure starvation looks us in the face. I do not mind it; but how can I see the children starve? I have never disturbed you in your studies; but pinched by this poverty I am forced to break my silence. Can you not stir yourself to drive the wolf of hunger from our door? You are a great Pandit with vast learning. Why do you not seek the presence of the Emperor Akbar, who is a great lover of learning? He will reward you, if you write something very fine for him."

The Brahman was aroused from his reveries. He felt he had neglected his household duties too long, being absorbed in his studies. So he began to write a poem with much care. The poem being finished, he set out with it for the Emperor's Palace, and managed somehow to send it up to His Majesty.

Emperor Akbar was very much struck with the

verses, and he at once sent for the writer and conferred on him the highest honour, namely, having him seated next to him. The Brahman was so gratified that he forgot all about his poverty and starving family. He heartily

THE GATE OF AN INDIAN PALACE.

thanked the Emperor for his kind appreciation of his learning and took leave. Akbar ordered a domestic to take one of his rich embroidered robes and give it to the Brahman. The man went after him with the robe, but the latter was so much elated that he ran rather than walked and, when he had come near his house, called out: " Brahmani,* Brahmani, never has a man met with more success ! "

The Brahmani who thought that success meant reward in gold coins, came out with a large vessel to receive them.

* The wife of a Brahman.

" The Emperor has bestowed upon me what has not fallen to the lot of any other man," said the Pandit.

" But you come empty handed ! " said his wife. " Where is the load ? Is it following ? "

" What do you mean by a load and that vessel ? The great Akbar has honoured me with a seat next to his, higher than any man's in the Kingdom. Don't you understand ? "

" I mean that we are on the verge of starvation and I want some money to buy food with. You are making a song of your honour, but that does not appease hunger ! Does it ? "

The Brahman stopped short. His elation was gone. Honour looked very small before the pangs of poverty.

Just then the domestic arrived with the rich robe, and presenting it to the Brahman as a royal gift, salaamed and departed.

" Here then is a rich thing," said the Brahman. " Our poverty is gone."

" But don't you see ? " said the wife ; " what good is it to us ? How can you dispose of the royal robe ? Or, how can you wear it over your rags ? You are given a cloak, while a shirt is wanting. You must go and return it and ask for money instead, if you want to save the children from starving to death."

The Brahman saw no other way than to obey his wife. But bethinking himself of the difficulty of gaining access to the Imperial Court and of his recent honour, he donned the robe on his way. When he entered the city of Delhi, people took him for a mad man and began to pelt him. He ran away from the crowd only to be seized by the police who took him over to the Kotowal (the Police Officer) as a thief. The Kotowal who knew nothing of the royal favour bestowed upon the Brahman, committed him to custody for trial.

Now, Akbar, hearing from the domestic that the learned Brahman lived in a very poor condition, set out with some courtiers for the Brahman's cottage to do him the further honour of a visit, and to help him from poverty. When he reached the cottage he was so deeply moved by the pitiable condition of the Pandit's family, that he at once ordered thousands of labourers and artisans to be employed to build a good house for the family. He also sent money and ornaments and maids for the Brahmani and servants for the Brahman.

The house was built in a few days, and the Brahmani was now shining like a Begum with her jewels and attendants, but the Brahman was missing. Search was made for him in all directions till the Kotowal came to learn the facts. Afraid of incurring the Emperor's displeasure, he had the Brahman carried to a distant dense jungle and left there to be devoured by wild beasts. But, as luck would have it, he met a hermit in the woods who gave him shelter and guided him out of the forest.

Spent out and weary, the Brahman reached the village at nightfall and with a throbbing heart, full of fears for his family, he wended his way to his cottage.

But lo! the cottage was not there. A palatial

mansion had taken its place. Streaks of light were gleaming out from the splendid hall and peals of laughter and music greeted his ears.

The poor Brahman sank down in a bitter agony of mind. He pictured to himself all sorts of horrors befalling his dear Brahmani and his children. They must, he thought, have been sold as slaves or killed by some heartless usurper, and tears rolled down his placid face.

Now all her servants had had instructions from the Brahmani to look for a poor Pandit and, if found, to bring him up to her at once. So when one of them perceived him in that woe-begone condition, he went up to a maid and asked her to report to their mistress, that a wretched thing somewhat resembling a Pandit was lying and lamenting near the outer gate.

As soon as the Brahmani heard this, she sallied out with her maids to welcome the Brahman. But when the Brahman saw her sailing towards him with her rustling silk *sari* and her tinkling ornaments, he rose to run away; but his legs would not carry him. By the orders of the Brahmani the maids seized him; but frantic with rage, he would not listen to the Brahmani's words. He struggled hard to free himself and cried :—

" Hands off, women. Do you not know that I should not touch any woman but my Brahmani? It is a sin."

" Then behold your Brahmani here." Saying this the Brahmani caught hold of him.

" Monster," cried the enraged Brahman. " You have driven away my Brahmani and children as homeless beggars and now you mock me with your cursed welcome. This is more than I can bear. I scorn your wealth and I spurn you. I would rather die than cross the threshold of your house."

The Brahmani dragged in her fatigued husband who was cursing, struggling, and kicking all the time. In the hall the Brahman was forced to deposit himself on a cushion. Then his wife threw off all her jewels and rich apparel; and attired in her old tattered rags, she addressed the Brahman thus :—

" Look, do you now recognise me ? "

The Brahman looked at her aghast.

" Now, hear what I say. It is all the work of the good Emperor, who has kindly made us rich. Oh ! what a painful time we have spent in finding you. Where have you been ? "

The Brahman thought a moment and then spoke :—

" Why have you accepted all this ? Do you not know the ways of a Brahman ? We are not to accept anything beyond what we want for bare existence. So send back these servants and riches to Akbar with our grateful thanks, but say that we shall be far more satisfied if we get only a cottage and a regular supply of bare necessaries. This wealth is no good to us. The worries of wealth will take off all the happiness of our simple life. So give it up."

The Brahmani answered, " You are my husband and I am in duty bound to obey you in all your wishes ,so your will be done."

The good Emperor was struck by the Pandit's proposal and did as he wished, revering him all the more for his grand self-denial.

THE MAGIC CHEST

IN India it is binding upon all men to be dutiful to their old parents. They should not only look after the comforts of their father and mother, but try to make them happy in every way. But there are " black as well as white sheep " among the Indian people and my story is about some bad sons.

An old man gave away all his money to his three sons, hoping, of course, that they would look after his happiness and comfort in his old age. But alas, his hopes were not fulfilled, for the sons and their wives looked after themselves, never caring to think of him save as an unnecessary burden—a hanger-on. The poor old man sorely felt the daily acts of negligence and insult and wrote to one of his nephews complaining of his sons' inhuman treatment. In a few days the nephew arrived with a big iron chest and declared that it contained all the money he could amass by investing the amount he had got from his uncle. Then he entrusted the key to his old uncle, saying, " You have once come to grief by giving away your money to your sons. Now take care that not a single coin of the chest be given to anybody till after your death. Keep the key always to yourself, and send word to me when you feel your death approaching." The nephew then took leave; but the chest he left had a magic effect on the old man's sons and daughters-in-law. They seemed, all of a sudden, to recollect that the father was the head of the family, who deserved their utmost care and devotion. So, better times dawned upon the poor old man. Sitting on the chest with a tremendous key dangling at the end of his trouser-girdle he now began to receive the attention and flattery of his relatives day and night. The wives of his sons vied with each other in serving him to win his favour. But being too much looked after he soon fell ill; and when it became doubtful whether he would recover, the sons pressed him hard to do something towards the disposal of the money he had in his chest. The old man, however, would do nothing till his nephew came and advised him. The nephew was accordingly sent for, and on his arrival his cousins asked him to induce their father to distribute the money in the chest while he was alive. But the nephew would not allow it to be opened till their father was dead and his funeral ceremony was celebrated in a fitting manner. He, however, made the old man provide that whatever the chest contained should be equally distributed among the three sons before a Panch.* At last he died and his nephew took great care to see that the chest was not touched till the funeral was duly gone through; but no sooner was it over than all the three sons rushed for the chest and

* Five, *e.g.* the Headmen of a community.

demanded the key from their cousin before the Panch of the village.

"Cousins mine," he said, "I have nothing more to do with the chest. The treasure in it is yours and you have got to share it equally. Good-bye."

Saying this he handed them the key, mounted upon a horse and rode away.

The three brothers then fell upon the chest, opened the lock, and with much difficulty raised the lid. They were on tiptoe of delight, expecting to find a hoard of blazing coins inside the chest. But to their horror and utter disappointment they found it full of rubbish and old shoes* made into three separate garlands. They became furious and were, in a fit of rage, going to throw away the contents. But the Panch and the neighbours compelled them to share the things equally and made them wear the garlands of shoes. One thing, however, could not be divided. It was the earthen bowl in which the poor old man was given his gruel before the arrival of the blessed (and afterwards cursed) chest. But his grandson, the only issue of the three brothers, came forward and claimed it, saying :—

"I must keep it to feed my papa from, when he will be old like dead grandpapa."

* Old shoes are held to be lucky in the west and are thrown after newly wedded couples for luck. But in India nothing is more insulting than touching a person with, or throwing at him, shoes—old or new.

A FOOL'S PARADISE.

A PANDIT accompanied by a barber, who acted as his servant, visited several cities in order to extend his knowledge as well as earn money by the display of his great learning. Travelling through many parts of the country, they arrived at a town where everything was sold at one price. The Pandit wondered how it could be possible, but seeing a little more of the town and the people, he came to the conclusion that they and their ruler, though good and active, were utterly devoid of sense. So he told the barber that it was unsafe to live in a place where people were deprived of reason.

He said :—" Dark is the town and the king blind : vegetables and sweets sell at the same price.* We must not live here. Let us leave at once."

But the barber loved sweets, and would not leave the town. Seeing that it was useless to remonstrate with his hare-brained companion, the Pandit went away alone, leaving the address of the place he was going to, with instructions that the barber should inform him in case he was in trouble.

The barber was delighted to be left at a place where everything was so cheap. He was doing himself well with the small earnings he made by shaving, till one day, all of a sudden, he was seized and carried into the presence of the Raja. A criminal, about to be burnt on the pile, being

* (Hindi) " *Andheri Nagari, Andhá Rájá*
Taká seer Bháji Taká Seer Khájá."
Taká —½ penny : *seer* — 2 lbs.

found too thin to burn brightly, the barber's portly person was deemed a good substitute. When brought before the Raja, he prayed hard for the execution to be delayed for one day, and his prayer was granted. He lost no time in

MESSENGER SENT TO THE PANDIT

sending a friend of his post-haste to the Pandit informing him of his danger.

Next day when everything was ready for the burning of the barber alive, the crowd's attention was drawn to a holy man who came running at full speed and crying :—

"Hold, stop, wait, this must not be. No one but myself shall ascend that pile."

It was the Pandit, and people wondered what he meant.

The Raja rose to receive him and asked him what his wishes were. The Pandit replied :—

"You must not waste time. Mount me on that pile and set fire to it within one hour—or the lucky time will pass away. I have been studying astronomy and the mystic sciences all these years in quest of a lucky hour in which to die and go to heaven. My calculations show that anybody who will be burnt on that pile at this hour will go straight to heaven. The combination of the stars and the merit of the pile will have this particular effect. So make haste, do not waste time. Burn me on the pile."

The Raja, who heard this, spoke out :—
"That cannot be. I will not allow anybody to use this burning pile in order to go to heaven. It is I who will avail myself of this opportunity. So let me be immolated on yonder pile without delay."

When the Raja was preparing to get on the pile, his mother came out and said, "Son, you cannot go to heaven before me. My claims are prior, so you must let me be burnt on the pile."

In India mothers are respected above all, so the Raja had to yield to her wishes. People cheered the Mother Rani when she ascended the pile and made straight for heaven.

The Pandit went off with the barber and hastened away from the Raja's territory.

"Now, fool," he said, "did you realise what I said to you? Fools only would like to live in a fool's paradise. But for me you must have perished."

A GRASS WIDOW'S HUSBAND

BHOLARAM was very stupid, although he was married. His widowed mother fell sick and asked him to go and fetch his wife from her village. At first Bohlaram would not go, but being pressed by his mother, he consented.

"I am old and I am sick," said his mother. "Your wife is now quite old enough to keep a house, so she must come and help me. Take some boy as your servant and have this rupee. You must buy something on your way to give to your wife."

Bholaram chose one of his playmates, Dhapole Ram, to accompany him. He was, of course, as dull as Bholaram himself, but he was quite willing to go with him as his servant.

They then set out and stopped at the first shop on their way. It chanced to be a cloth shop, and Bholaram took a piece of cloth for his wife, such as is worn by widows only.

They then walked on till they came in view of the village in which Bholaram's wife lived with her father and other relatives. Bholaram plodded on, but the nearer he came to his father-in-law's house the more nervous he became. He was very shy and could not look anybody in the face excepting his mother and playmates. So he was quite upset at the idea of having to face so many people whom he had not seen for a long time.

"Dhapole Ram," said he, "I swear by you,* my heart is throbbing and my legs trembling. I cannot, I cannot go to that house. You must

* Indicates the importance of the person spoken to.

go with the cloth and say that it has been sent my wife by my mother who wants her to come and live with her. I'll wait here, but never, never, say a word about me."

Dhapole Ram also feared to meet new people, but he at last summoned up courage to take the cloth alone. The first person he met was a maid of the house. He handed her the cloth and sent the message by her. Soon after he heard loud cries of mourning inside the house. He asked a man, who came out, what the matter was, and gathered from his reply that Bholaram's wife had become a widow. So he ran with this dreadful news to where Bholaram was waiting.

" Master Bholaram, Master Bholaram," he cried. " Your wife has become a widow. They are all lamenting inside the house."

" Ah ! " said Bholaram, " then we must hurry back and inform my mother."

They came back as fast as their legs could carry them, and as soon as Bholaram reached home, he cried out to his mother :—

" Ma, Ma, there is sad news for you."

The mother hurried out of her sick bed and asked " What, is your wife dead ? "

" Not dead," said Bholaram, " she has become a widow."

" You foolish boy," said the mother. " You have been a fool all your life. Now can your wife be a widow when you are alive ? "

" Come, come," retorted the boy. " Don't be foolish yourself. If my living prevents anybody from being a widow, how could you become one ? "

ADVENTURES OF A JAMAI* (IN BENGAL)

CHUNI RAM had to go to his father-in-law's house,† but he did not know how to talk politely with people. His mother gave him a full course of training on the eve of his departure. Some of her lessons ran as follows :—

"When you are talking to a gentleman, you first ask his name, then, his father's name and his grandfather's name and so on. Then you ask him if he is married and if he has any children. Then you turn the conversation to some object of interest near at hand, and express your wish to know the particulars. Do not sit on the floor but on some high seat. When you meet the ladies of the house do not speak in your gruff voice, but try to make it as soft and sweet as possible. Do not eat much, refuse some courses, and do not praise dainties too much. Say that I often treat you to them. Note and remember the special dishes to report them to me."

* Son-in-law.

† In India child-marriage is still in vogue among many communities. But a married girl generally lives with her father till she attains a certain age. In the meantime both the bride and the bridegroom are invited to their respective father-in-law's house every now and then, and are entertained by their relations. In some parts of the country the bride does not visit her husband's house till she attains a certain age, and *gawanawa*—a sort of second marriage—is celebrated.

ADVENTURES OF A JAMAI (IN BENGAL)

When Chuni Ram arrived at his father-in-law's house the latter welcomed him cordially, and expressed his delight at seeing him after such a long time. Chuni Ram who remembered his mother's instructions too well, at once assailed him with the questions :—" What is your father's name ? " " What is your grand-father's name ? " " What is your great grand-father's name ? " " What is your caste ? " " What is your *gotra* (clan) ? "* " Where is your dwelling place ? " etc.

The father-in-law kept answering these questions thinking that Chuni Ram might not have recognised him. He sought for an opportunity to explain that he was the father-in-law. So, when Chuni Ram asked :—

" Are you married ? "

He replied : " How could you marry my daughter if I were not ? "

Chuni Ram : " Still there is no harm in asking the question."

Father-in-Law : " Yes, I am married."

Chuni : " Have you any children ? "

Father-in-Law : " Your wife is a daughter of mine."

Chuni : " Yet I only ask the question."

Father-in-Law : " I have only two daughters and three sons."

Then Chuni Ram, seeing that a river was running hard by, asked :—

" Where does this river flow to ? "

* Men of the olden days used to open conversation with strangers with such questions. But now they would start a conversation by such makeshifts as reference to the weather, as in Europe, or request for the loan of matches, etc., etc.

Father-in-Law: " To the sea."

Chuni: " Who dug this river ? "

Father-in-Law: " No one, the river flows naturally."

Chuni: " What has become of the earth ? "

The father-in-law could not stand such foolish questions any longer, and in a fit of anger he said:

" Half of the earth has been eaten by your parents and half by myself."

Chuni: " How is that ? "

Father-in-Law: " How else could a son be born like yourself, and how else could I choose such a son-in-law as you ? "

With this he called a maid to take the Jamai to the Zenana* and walked away muttering in disgust.

Chuni Ram was conducted to the sitting-room of the ladies, and was asked to sit down. He at once remembered his mother's instructions to occupy some high seat. So he settled himself on the top of a cupboard which he found to be the highest, and which he scaled up with difficulty. Presently his mother-in-law† appeared and was taken aback to see her Jamai perched up on a cupboard. Before she could speak, Chuni Ram uttered :—

" Coo-oo, coo-oo," in imitation of a cuckoo, remembering his mother's advice to make his voice as soft and sweet as possible. His mother-in-law thinking that he had gone mad, ran away.

* Ladies' apartments.

† Young married couples seldom meet before others. In many parts of India even the mother-in-law would not appear before nor speak to the son-in-law.

ADVENTURES OF A JAMAI (IN BENGAL)

Chuni Ram was having his dinner with his brothers-in-law. The ladies* of the house and neighbourhood stood by the Jamai to joke with him, and to press him to eat. Unfortunately Chuni Ram was night-blind†—seeing very little after dusk. But he was very loath to confess it. So he refused many dishes without seeing them. When pressed to eat different courses he said :—

"My mother often treats me to it."

Now it so happened that a cat was eating out of Chuni Ram's plate unmolested.‡ Being night-blind he could not see it. One of the girls said in jest :—

"Has not the Jamai eyes to see that the cat is sharing with him his food like another Jamai?"

Chuni Ram was vexed to know that a cat was taking advantage of his defective sight, and said :—

"Never mind, I shall give it a sound lesson presently."

Just then Chuni Ram's mother-in-law came to serve some rice-pudding. Chuni Ram, thinking that the cat had again started eating from his plate, aimed a blow in the direction of the noise as hard as he could. The poor mother-in-law was sent spinning on the floor, and her plate and pudding flew right in the face of Chuni Ram. Along with the plate and pudding

* Ladies in India generally have their meals after the men have been served.

† Nyctalopia. This disease is uncommon in England but common in India. People suffering from it can see things in daytime, but they become blind when it is dark.

‡ The Indians have their meals on the floor.

came blows from the brothers-in-law, who were furious at seeing their mother so brutally treated. But the kind old woman checked her sons and said :—

"Don't treat him ill. It is not his fault. He is off his head." Then she left the room after asking the other ladies to see that all went well. In due course, the dinner came to an end, and all but Chuni Ram left their seats. Seeing Chuni Ram not moving, the ladies asked if he would have something more to eat. He would neither eat nor move—the former because he had too much pudding taken through his eyes, nostrils and mouth, and the latter because he could not see his way about. Chuni Ram's not moving moved his mother-in-law to pity. She came and asked him not to mind what had happened. She then took him by the hand, led him to his bedroom, and gave him a wash and change of dress.

Chuni Ram was sleeping with his wife ; but in the small hours of the morning he woke up and felt he must have a pull at his hookka.* But it was necessary to get fire from the cow-shed for this and it was yet dark ; so Chuni Ram devised a plan for going out and retracing his steps without letting his wife know of his night-blindness. He felt for the well-rope and when he got it he tied one end of it round his body and the other end to one of the legs of the bed. Then he felt for the door and in a few minutes was out in the courtyard. He crossed the yard

* Hookka—hubble-bubble. A big Indian pipe for smoking.

and when he was in the cowshed, a bull struck him with its horns. As he was rushing away to escape the bull he tumbled against the low wall of the well in a corner of the yard and fell into it. His struggles to get out of the well with the aid of the rope gave some hard jerks to the bed in which his wife was sleeping. She was awakened by the shaking and cried out for help, thinking that she was disturbed by some ghost. The rest of the household dashed into the room with lighted wicks, and were amazed to see that the Jamai was not in bed, and that the bed was moving by itself. Naturally they ascribed this to some unearthly agency and supposed that the Jamai had been spirited away. But someone detected the rope tied to one of the legs of the bedstead, and at once drew the attention of others to it. They all traced the rope to the well and found Chuni Ram dangling at the end of it inside the well. They thought that he was attempting to commit suicide out of remorse and shame. So they dragged him out and compelled him to go to bed again, giving him another change of dress.

The next morning found Chuni Ram returning home.

Among the things he had eaten at his father-in-law's house, he had particularly enjoyed some cocoanut cakes. So all the way home he was saying: "Cocoanut cakes, cocoanut cakes," in order to remember the name to mention it to his mother. Not far away from his house there was a tank where he washed his hands and feet, and put on his shoes.* In the meantime he had forgotten his "cocoanut cakes," so he cried out: "Oh, I have lost it—I have lost it."

Some people hard by thought that he had lost something very precious. So they at once began to dive into the tank to find the lost treasure. The number was increased by new-comers. Chuni Ram sat disconsolate near the brink of the water trying his best to recollect the name, when a cocoanut fell with a thud from a tree near the tank. He was startled by the noise, but a man said: "It is only a cocoanut."

Chuni Ram cried out: "I have got it. I have got it," and ran as hard as he could towards his house, fearing to be benighted on the way—for the sun had set and it was getting dark. The people who were diving for the lost treasure of Chuni Ram were very much enraged at having got nothing in return for their trouble. So they got out of the water and ran after him. Presently he found an ox, belonging to his parents, grazing in the field, and seeing no other way of getting home after nightfall, he caught hold of its tail. The ox dragged him through bushes and brambles and never stopped till it reached the cowshed.

On hearing the noise Chuni Ram's mother came out to see what made the ox so restive, and was amazed to see her son hanging by its tail—his clothes all torn to pieces and his skin

* Many village-people of Bengal carry their shoes while walking over boggy lands, and put them on when they are near their destination. Some would do it to avoid as much wear and tear to the shoes as possible.

all scratched by thorns and bleeding. Just then arrived the party of peasants who had dived to find Chuni Ram's lost treasure, and who angrily demanded a reward or Chuni Ram's person. At the same time a messenger arrived from Chuni Ram's father-in-law with a letter to the effect that he would rather die than acknowledge Chuni Ram as his son-in-law. There was a great sensation in the village and people flocked to hear of Chuni Ram's adventures.

IDIOTIC KALIDAS

TRADITION says that Kalidas, the greatest poet of India, was in his youth an absolute dunce. The King of the province in which he lived had an exceptionally accomplished daughter. She made up her mind to marry nobody who was not young and at the same time superior to her in scholarship. Suitor after suitor of the highest attainments paid their addresses to her, but none could satisfactorily answer the scholastic questions of the princess. The King's patience was exhausted and he summoned a Council of the most learned men of his kingdom and asked them to manage to have his proud and obstinate daughter married to an idiot.

The learned men were in search of an idiot when they found Kalidas seated on the branch of a tree which he was cutting. He sat on the end of the branch and was cutting it towards the trunk, so that he was sure to fall down with the branch on its being severed from the tree.

The Pandits admitted that he was the greatest dunce, and they required him to come down and follow them. Before he was taken to the Court as a suitor for the princess's hand, he was tutored by the Pandits to shake his head or make some signs in answer to her questions. So Kalidas only shook his head or made some signs when the princess questioned him, while the learned men answered her as if by way of explaining his gestures.

All the Court were loud in admiration of the newcomer's wisdom, which could be interpreted only by the biggest Pandits ; and the Princess also accepted the verdict.

The nuptials were performed and at night when Kalidas was conducted to the Princess' bedroom, he did not know how to get to the bed —as the curtains were all drawn. He devised a means to scale up one of the bedstead posts and then clambered on to the canopy of the bed. Down came he with the curtains on the Princess, who was in bed and screamed out for help. Kalidas was confused and made haste to hide himself underneath the bedstead. The domestics rushed in and after some search found him. Having adjusted matters they left the married couple to themselves.

Kalidas was still mute, but the princess forced him to speak. The first word he spoke was mispronounced and the second word was more so. The princess then perceived the deception played on her and kicked Kalidas out of the room.

Kalidas was going to drown himself. But, as the tradition goes, the Goddess of Learning took pity on him and gifted him with faculties that made him the greatest poet of India.

THE LUXURY OF HAVING TWO WIVES

SOMETIMES a man in India will indulge in the luxury of having two or more wives. Such a one was Mani Ram, being blessed with two. The elder wife was named Kasturi and the younger Kaisar.

One night Mani Ram was tired, and asked Kasturi to massage his body a little.

Kasturi said: "Kaisar is your favourite. You never tell her to do anything. Poor me!"

Kaisar could not bear this, and interrupted:

"What business have you to say that, you spiteful wretch? You will not stir even to carry a straw from one place to another. Yet you mean to say that I do nothing. You get on my nerves."

Kasturi made a scathing reply; an altercation between the co-wives gradually led to a tempestuous quarrel; and then they closed in a hand-to-hand (rather hand-in-hair) fight. Mani Ram begged first one and then the other to cease, but neither heeded him. He then fell between the two, and the massaging business was half finished by the blows he received from them.

When the speed of the blows had slowed down a little, Mani Ram again made his piteous appeal to both to cease quarrelling, and to have half and half of his body for the massaging purpose. But a dispute arose as to which of them should have the right side and which the left. Both of them rushed for the right part of the body, and Mani Ram's right arm was nearly torn off before he could free it from their firm grips. He then proposed that they should have

THE LUXURY OF HAVING TWO WIVES.

both parts of his body turn by turn. Again the question arose which of them should begin with the right, and Mani Ram was again subjected to a tussle for a good length of time. Spent with jostling, he at last offered the reward of a trinket to the one who would take up the left part. Now the tugging operation commenced on the left side.

Mani Ram was at his wits' end, and the endless jostling meant the end of his life. He at last bethought himself of the fact that Kasturi liked, and Kaisar disliked a particular scent. His offer of a trinket was then at once changed; and he said that the wife who would begin with the left part of his body should have a present of that particular *ittar*. Kasturi who was awfully fond of the *ittar* accepted the offer, but Kaisar who hated it did not care for the reward, and took up the right side of her husband for massaging.

The wives had not made much progress in their work, before they picked another quarrel. Kaisar had transgressed the line dividing Mani Ram's body into the right and left parts.

"How dare you," said Kasturi, "put your dirty hand on the part belonging to me?"

Kaisar: "You call my hand dirty? Here you are." Saying this she brought the palm of her left hand with a thud on Mani Ram's left side.

Kasturi: "You strike my part? Then here you are," and a heavy blow descended on the right side.

Kaisar: "Oh, you wretch! you deal blows? Do you? Then I must kick."

Mani Ram's left side got the promised kick in a moment.

Kasturi: "If you kick my part once I shall kick yours thrice."

The promised vengeance was not slow to follow. And this was retaliated with double the number of kicks by the rival. Then came kick after kick from both the wives, fiercely enraged by the insult they fancied they received at the hands—or the feet rather—of each other. In their excitement they took no notice of the pain and cries of their *dear dear* husband. Poor Mani Ram was trying to get up, but was prevented by the shower of kicks which went on till he began to writhe in pain and cry for help.

Now a thief, who had come to steal, lurked in a corner of the house, and was waiting for the hour when the husband and wives would go to bed and be fast asleep. He had waited and watched for about three hours, when the cries of the wretched husband collected neighbours all round the house. So he could not make good his escape and was easily seized—people think ing that it was he who was the cause of the alarm.

When the thief was taken before the Kotowal* he said :—

" Of course you will punish me, but pray give me any other punishment than that of having two wives."

" What do you mean ? " asked the Kotowal.

The thief then related the whole story to the amusement of all present, and as a reward for the tale he was let free.

* Police Superintendent.

"MUSIC HATH CHARMS"

THERE lived in a village a poor youth who loved to sing. He would sing in season and out of season, though his voice was unbearably squeaky. It was a dreadful ordeal to listen to the shrill piercing noise when he *brayed* out his rhymeless and tuneless music. His father and mother tried their best to cure him of his passion for singing, but to no effect. They then hit on the plan of turning him out into the street the moment he opened his lips to sing. The boy gave his lungs free exercise in the street till the neighbours got tired of his songs. They came out in a body with clubs and sticks and chased the boy away. Finding the village too hot for him, he repaired to the woods and sang to his heart's content under the shade of a tree. He indulged in this for some time, when a spirit, who lived in the tree, appeared before him and cried out: "O, shut up* your caterwauling. I am sick of it."

"Now, look here," said the boy, "they will not let me sing at home, neither in the street, nor on the outskirts of the village. So I come here

* Many slang phrases like this are the charms of the English language: and the author begs pardon for his offence against the rules of polite literature if he yields to the irresistible temptation to use such phrases.

to sing my songs and even you come down to stop me! This is too bad; I must have a place where I can use my gift; therefore, I am not going to be stopped here."

But the spirit had had enough of his talent and would have no more of it. So to get rid of his noise he made him an offer. "Listen to me," he said. "If you cease inflicting your music on me I will give you a reward. I am going to enter into the body of your landlord's daughter and won't come forth until you go and try to cure her. Your success in exorcising her will bring you money."

With much reluctance the boy accepted the terms, and waited and waited till the news of the girl's falling ill was in everybody's mouth. They said she was suffering from a strange malady which no physician could cure. The boy went up to the landlord and said, "I will cure your daughter, my lord." He was at first laughed at; but as they say "A drowning man catches at a straw," the hopeless father at last allowed him to try. As pre-arranged the spirit left the girl as soon as the boy made his appearance and she gradually got better. The boy had his reward and went home. He would daily walk out to a lonely spot in another part of the forest and start his singing. Birds and animals left the place, scared away by his voice; so he went on unmolested.

Now, it so happened that the same spirit entered into the Princess of a neighbouring country. The boy, whose name was now known to fame, was sought after and brought to the

Court to treat the Princess. The spirit who intended not to meet the boy any more, was very angry at seeing him come to treat the Princess.

"What evil wind blows you here, my boy?" said the spirit. "You have no business here."

"My business here," answered the boy, "is to ask you to leave the Princess this very moment."

"Tut," said the spirit, "I agreed to give you one chance only, and I am not going to give you another; so leave me in peace and don't attempt to cross my path again."

"Well, I shall *Sing* then!" cried the boy defiantly.

"Pray don't, don't," cried the spirit. "Oh no, no, I cannot stand it—I will leave at once." So the spirit left not only the Princess but the country for good. The boy had now a good time of it in his part of the forest where he was free to enjoy the practice of his favourite art.

BUTTER WINS THE DAY

A KING had two favourite domestics, Kalu and Chameli, husband and wife. The couple lived in peace for a long time, but one day they fell out over a cow. They had no cow but they were proposing to buy one.

"I shall love the cow," said the wife Chameli, "and the nice little calf she will give us."

"I shall love the milk," said the husband Kalu, "and the cream if you make any."

"But how can you have milk and cream when I am going to give you neither? I must make butter and buttermilk, and none but my dear little calf will have the milk."

"You are not going to have your own way in this matter," growled the husband.

"Why not, when I shall have all the work of looking after the cow and calf?"

"Certainly not. I love milk and milk I must have."

The quarrel went on in this strain till they agreed on a plan to decide if they should have milk or butter. Both of them went to bed and covered themselves with blankets, agreeing that the one who first made the slightest movement or utterance should lose in the dispute. They doggedly kept still and silent, forgetting all about their duties at the palace.

The king and queen finding their domestics absent too long, sent for them. The man who went to fetch Kalu and Chameli shouted to them at the top of his voice, but they would neither stir nor speak. He hastened to the palace to report that Kalu and Chameli had both died.

The Royal Consorts were grieved at the sad news and ordered the funeral of the couple. Thus Kalu and Chameli were put on biers wrapped as they had been in their blankets, and were carried to the place where dead bodies were burnt. Yet they would not move or speak. The King then thought he would go himself and make sure of the cause of their death. So he went to the place and declared he would give a reward of a hundred rupees to the man who could tell him the truth as to the sudden death of Kalu and Chameli.

"The truth is, my lord," cried out Kalu, springing to his feet, "that I am dying for milk and my wife for butter. Let me have my reward."

Just then Chameli rushed in from the bier and shouted out: "I have won, he has lost. No milk, only butter."

All present fled, fearing that the ghosts of the dead had risen. But Kalu and Chameli ran after them, the former demanding his reward, and the latter exulting in her victory for butter.

Note—In Bengal the story goes that the bone of contention between a Brahman and a Brahmani was three *Koi* fish. Either of them wanted two, and would give the other the odd one. Thus they had a big quarrel and acted as the characters of the above story.

A CLEVER PHYSICIAN

THERE was a very clever Hakim (physician) who was renowned for his skill in discovering anything wrong with the body by merely feeling the pulse.

One day when he called upon a patient, he was attended by one of his pupils, who was very eager to learn the Hakim's art of detecting a man's complaints. So he was all attention when his teacher was examining the sick-man.

The Hakim first looked about the patient's room and then sat by his bed and began to feel his pulse. After he had done so he grew very cross and said :—

" How can you hope to get better, when you do not act upon my advice ? I told you not to eat any sour things, but you have eaten an orange ! "

The patient at first denied, but being told that he would suffer more if he did not tell the truth, he admitted that he had eaten an orange.

The pupil was struck with wonder at the miraculous skill of his teacher. When they had left the patient's house the pupil pressed the physician hard to explain how he could know, by feeling the pulse, that the patient had eaten an orange.

"Didn't you see, you fool, that I examined the room first and found orange peel under the patient's bed? Now, any man with a grain of sense could conclude that the patient had eaten an orange."

The pupil bore this in mind, and when he set up as an independent physician and went to attend a patient, he first took a survey of the room and found a panther skin under the patient's bed. He became furious and said, "How can you get better when you have eaten a panther?"

The patient was astounded and said, "No, sir, I never ate a panther."

"Come, now," said the physician, "no mincing of facts with a Hakim, speak out the truth."

The patient's patience was exhausted and he ordered the Hakim to be bundled out.

FISHING FOR THE MOON

ONE night there was a festival in the village of Baglolegáon. The villagers gathered together at the landlord's house to make merry at a drinking bout. They were far gone in liquor when a man broke in with the news that he had found a plate of living gold shining in the river. The landlord was at once seized with the desire of possessing it. So he, at the head of all his party, proceeded to the spot where the great discoverer led them. "Look," said this man, pointing to the moonbeams in the river, "Look, did I tell you a lie? Is it not gold?"

"Certainly, certainly," cried all, and the landlord ordered the fishermen of the village to cast nets to fish it out. Eventually they set to work and caught many fish but not the gold plate. The plate kept shifting its place with the decline of the moon and finally disappeared altogether as the moon set. But the people of Baglolegáon thought that the gold dish had sunk deep into the water, and their progeny still cast nets and dive down to the river bed in the hope of finding the precious piece of gold.

"HOIST WITH YOUR OWN PETARD"

THERE is quite as much trickery in selling elephants in India as is practised by horse-dealers in western countries. At a great elephant-fair in Northern Bengal a dealer was showing a pair of elephants to a zemindar (landlord). At a critical point in the bargaining between them, the dealer saw a simple peasant approach the elephant and narrowly examine a part of his gigantic frame. Fearing that the intruder would "crab the deal," he took advantage of the zemindar's momentary absence to consult his servants, and slipped ten rupees into the rustic's willing palm. Then his customer returned and agreed to purchase the animal.

After the exchange was agreed upon, the dealer whispered to the peasant, "I say, how did you find out what was wrong with my elephant? I saw you spotting his one defect."

"Brother," answered the peasant, "I was wondering what the huge thing was, and was feeling it simply to make sure whether it was made of wood or stone. But I found out to my astonishment that the stupendous mass is a living animal of flesh and blood."

A LAME SCRIBE

A PEASANT, who did not know how to read and write, once went to a man and asked him to write a letter for him. The letter was to be addressed to his landlord who lived in a town not very far off.

"I cannot write your letter," said the man, "for I have got a bad leg."

"Sir," said the peasant, "I do not know much, but I cannot see what a bad leg has to do with writing a letter."

"It has much to do," said the man, "for I cannot walk the whole distance to go and read out the letter to your landlord."

"What do you mean, sir?" said the rustic. "My landlord knows how to read and there are men with him who can read. Why then need you go and read the letter for them?"

"Don't you see, you goose," replied the other man, "that none but myself can read the letters which I write?"

AN IDLE SERVANT

IT was night time; and in a bungalow a gentleman went to bed to sleep. His servant, Rama, was sleeping on the floor near his bed.

"Rama, Rama," cried the master. "Will you see if it is raining outside?"

Rama could only be roused with difficulty and his master had to repeat the question several times. Then Rama, having rubbed his eyes, yawned twice or thrice and snapped his fingers, replied:—

"It is raining, master."

"How do you know?" asked his master.

"The cat came in," answered Rama.

"But how does a cat's coming in prove that it is raining?"

"I felt its coat, sir," said Rama, "and it was wet."

"All right!" said the master, "will you put out the lamp? I cannot sleep with the light."

"Well, sir," said Rama, "you need but cover your face with the sheet and you will find it dark."

"You are a lazy fellow," said the master. "Come, shut the door."

"Master," said Rama, "I have done two things for you. Now it is your turn to do the third."

Saying this Rama turned over and went to sleep again and soon began to snore.

A SERVANT'S PHILOSOPHY

A MAN, who was sick, told his servant to go to a doctor and get him some medicine.

"The doctor may not be in his dispensary," the servant said.

"Go and see, he must be there," said the master.

"It is true he may be there, but he may not give me the medicine," said the servant.

"He will give it," said the master, "for he left a few minutes ago saying that he would give the medicine to any man I might send to him."

"It is also true he may give me the medicine, sir, but it may not have any effect," said the servant.

"It must have some effect," said the master, "the doctor assured me of it."

"What if it has effect?" said the servant, "you have to die some day and the medicine will not prevent you from dying."

It was a pity that this far-sighted servant was dismissed for his wise views.

THE FORESIGHT OF A SERVANT

A GENTLEMAN had a very stupid servant. He once bade him wash the floor of his room. The servant in his over-zeal to please the master washed the walls as well, and thus spoilt the paint and decorations. The gentleman got very angry and told him never to do things beyond his actual orders. After some time the servant was asked to light a fire in the bedroom, so that the smoke might drive the mosquitoes out. When the fire was lit, a high wind was blowing which scattered the sparks all over the room. Soon the curtains caught fire and a part of the house was burnt down. The gentleman was again very angry with his servant and demanded :—

" Why did you not put out the fire when the wind was so high ? "

" Master," replied the servant, " you told me only to *light* the fire and nothing more. I carried out your bidding to the letter, and I am not to blame if I did not venture to act beyond your order."

" But you see," rejoined the master, " you must exercise your common sense and try to foresee and meet possible events—I mean, happenings which are highly probable in the natural order of things."

The servant bore this instruction in mind; and when soon afterwards his master fell ill and he was asked to call in a doctor, he tried hard to *foresee the possible event.* The only thing that might happen in the natural order was, he thought, the death of his master. So on his way to the Doctor's house he made all arrangements for the funeral ceremonies.

Now, along with the Doctor came in the kinsmen and the bier with other materials for the carrying away and the burning of the dead body; and then came the party of mourners, beating their breasts and crying out in a rhythmical bewailing.* The Doctor after examining his patient said :—

"Your complaint is not at all serious. But what for is all this funeral arrangement?"

The gentleman, who was himself much surprised, asked his servant, "who has called all these people here?"

"It is I, master. You must now give me credit for foreseeing a possible happening. I have not left anything undone in order to meet the possible event of your death."

* In some parts of India (especially Gujarat) there is a system of hiring mourners who beat their breasts to a regular time and cry in a singsong chant.

A MISER'S SERVANT

A MISER was once invited by a friend of his to an after-dinner party. The friend's house was rather far off, and as the miser took good care never to pay for the luxury of a drive, he set out early to walk the distance. He nearly reached his destination when it struck him that he had forgotten to put out the lamp in his room. He turned back at once and ran towards his house as fast as he could to avoid the tremendous waste of oil that would be caused by the burning of the lamp. Having arrived at his front door he called out to his servant and asked if the lamp in his room was still burning. The servant replied that he could not be so negligent as to allow such a waste.

"But Master," he continued, "you must have been extravagant in allowing your shoes to be so much the more worn down by coming back."

"Look!" said the miser, with a tone of triumph. "Look, here are the shoes under my arms. You cannot teach your master a lesson in economy!"

TENALIRAM AND THE HUNCH-BACK

TENALIRAM, the famous Court Jester of the King of Vijaynagaram, once incurred the displeasure of his master. By the order of the King he was to be half-buried in the ground and then trampled on by an elephant.

Accordingly Tenaliram was led out of the city of Vijaynagaram and was buried breast-deep somewhere near a public road. But the elephant that was to tread on him suddenly became mad and made towards the crowd that had gathered. They were seized with panic and fled to a man; whereupon the elephant also ran away, being followed by the King's servants. Thus poor Tenaliram was left alone in this awful plight, trembling under the shadow of a terrible death.

Ere long there came a hunch-back, who was much surprised to find a man in such a pitiable state. He drew near Tenaliram and asked :—" What is the matter with you, friend? Who has buried you alive like that?"

" My dear friend," said Tenaliram, " nothing but a hunch is the matter with me. A physician has buried me thus, assuring me that my hump will be gone in one hour. But it is gone one hour and I am counting the minutes to his return. I am simply dying with impatience to see whether I have been made straight by this treatment."

The hunch-back was also very eager to know the result; and with Tenaliram's permission he set to work to dig him out with the tools left by the King's servants. When Tenaliram came out, he pretended to be overjoyed at seeing himself straight and burst into ecstatic praises of the physician's skilful device. Naturally the other man was very much impressed and was yearning to have his own hunch treated likewise. So he entreated Tenaliram to do him a friendly turn by burying him in the same way as he himself had been. Tenaliram was only too glad to do it and to make haste to depart, leaving the man in the hope that the physician would soon return and take care of him.

Tenaliram had not been gone long when the officers returned with another elephant to execute the King's command. But imagine their amazement at seeing a stranger buried in the place of the real culprit.

The buried hunch-back, addressing the head officer, said:—"Excuse me, Sir Physician, I have not been quite one hour yet since your patient put me in here. But you may drag me out to see if the hump on my back is all right. I must say I was not prepared for the honour you are going to do me by giving me a ride on the elephant in order to parade the success of your skilful treatment. I pity my predecessor who has deprived himself of it by hastening away. He said he could not wait, but he desired me to pay you his warmest thanks and compliments."

"Well," exclaimed the officer, "blow me if this is not about the limit! Take that man out and let him explain what he says."

In the meantime the King, whose anger against Tenaliram had cooled down, felt sorry that he had inflicted such a horrible punishment on his favourite jester. So he had a pleasant surprise when Tenaliram made his appearance before him. He was keenly eager to know how the victim of his wrath could have escaped the fate to which he had been doomed.

"Did I not say," answered Tenaliram, "that I bear a charmed life? Fire cannot burn me, water cannot melt me, the sea cannot drown me, and elephants cannot trample on me. I am proof against these, your Majesty."

The King was pondering deeply, when the officers arrived with the hunch-back and explained how Tenaliram had made off by playing a trick upon the poor deformed person.

The whole court was much amused to hear the story and the King readily granted Tenaliram his pardon.

A NOVEL WAY OF COOKING

A POOR Brahman who could not marry his daughter for want of money once applied to the Maharaja of Krisnanagar for assistance. The Maharaja had already been bothered by too many applications of this nature and had on many occasions been taken in by artful beggars with bogus claims to charity. So, he was in a vindictive mood, and seeing that the applicant could not be put off by ordinary means, he said:

"I will give the Brahman one thousand rupees if he can pass one night in the tank of cold water behind my palace, with nothing to warm him for nine hours."

The Brahman was really needy. So, cold as the month of January was, he agreed to be in the water for one night in order to win the large sum of money.

The Maharaja was nonplussed by the man's willingness to undergo such a severe ordeal. But he did not believe he would pass through it successfully and appointed sentries to keep watch on him while he was in the water.

Early the next morning the Maharaja was eager to know the result of the arrangement. He hoped the Brahman had failed in the attempt. But the watchman came and reported that he had stayed in the water for the whole night and had come out of it safe and sound in the morning.

"Is it possible?" asked the Maharaja.

"Yes, your Highness," answered the sentries, "there is no mistake about it. We kept a very strict watch."

Maharaja: "Are you sure there was no fire near by?"

Sentries: "No, your Highness."

Maharaja: "Nor any light?"

Sentries: "There was a light on the balcony of the palace, your Highness."

Maharaja: "Did not the Brahman look at it?"

Sentries: "Of course, he kept looking at it."

Maharaja: "Ah, now I see how he could manage to keep himself warm. Go and tell him that I am not going to pay him the money, for he has not fulfilled the condition. He availed himself of the warmth of the light on the balcony."

The poor Brahman was told what the Maharaja had said; and he was stunned, as it were, by the sad disappointment. He felt too miserable to walk and sat down by the palace gate.

The Court Jester, Gopal Bhánd, was on his way to the palace when his attention was drawn to the Brahman's woebegone condition. He asked the poor man the reason of his grief and was told all about the Maharaja's cruel treatment.

Gopal Bhánd consoled the Brahman and said, "If you come and stay at my house, I will make the Maharaja change his mind." The Brahman cheered up and was only too delighted to follow the Bhánd to his house.

Asking his people to look after the Brahman, the Bhánd went out in search of some labourers

A NOVEL WAY OF COOKING.

and a very long bamboo. When he got them he caused the bamboo to be erected in front of his out-house and placed a pot at the top of it. Then he made a fire at its foot and seated himself near it, feeding the fire to keep it ablaze.

The Maharaja missed his jester at his court

and sent for him. The man who went to summon the jester was struck by the unusual sight of a bamboo pole, a pot at its top, and a fire at its foot. He, however, concealed his amazement and gave the Maharaja's message.

"My dear fellow," said Gopal Bhánd, "tell his Highness I cannot come to the court just now. I am simply starving and I must have a feed before I can go out. My wife is not well, so I am cooking my own food."

The messenger hastened back and informed the court of his strange experience at Gopal Bhánd's house. Then the Maharaja asked some of the courtiers to go and see what the matter was with the jester. They also came back and reported the strange process of his cooking and concluded by saying :—

"Your Highness, there is no doubt that Gopal Bhánd has gone mad or he is possessed. There is no other explanation of his erratic action."

The Maharaja was very much surprised and went in person to see what had gone wrong with the jester.

Gopal Bhánd received the Maharaja with respect and said : "I am very sorry for the trouble I have caused your Highness. But you see I could not go before I had finished my cooking. I am too poor to keep a cook and my wife is indisposed, and so I am compelled to prepare food myself. However, I shall not be long. I will have only rice to-day and I am going to have it as soon as it is boiled."

Maharaja : "But where is the rice you are boiling ?"

Gopal Bhánd: "Why, the rice is in the pot at the top of the bamboo."

Maharaja: "Well, I never, if this does not cap all! How can you boil rice by this process of cooking? You stupid clown!"

Gopal Bhánd: "It is very easy to understand the process. You see, the pot with rice and water is there and the fire is here, and the heat of the fire goes straight up to the top of the bamboo and boils the rice there. Is it not clear to you?"

Maharaja: "You are certainly gone mad, Gopal Bhänd. How can the pot be heated at all by a fire at such a distance?"

Gopal Bhánd: "If a Raja goes mad, it is only in the fitness of things that his subjects should also go mad. If the light of a lamp on the balcony could warm the body of a man in the tank, my fire here certainly can heat the pot there."

Maharaja: "Ah! now I catch your meaning; you are never funny without a motive. Well, I am really very sorry for the Brahman, and I want to make amends for my unfair treatment of him. Can anyone find him?"

Gopal Bhánd had only to call out for the Brahman, who instantly appeared before all. The Maharaja ordered his treasurer to pay him two thousand rupees instead of one.

A SHARP RETORT

THERE was once a King who did not smoke and often took his courtiers to task for indulging in this bad habit. One day the King and the courtiers walked out into a field in which tobacco was grown. At one end of the field there stood a donkey, silently gazing at the leaves of the tobacco plants, but making no attempt to eat them.

"Look here," said the King, "tobacco is such a bad thing that *even* donkeys will have nothing to do with it."

"Pardon, your Majesty," retorted the court-jester Birbal, "it is only such stupid things as donkeys that do not enjoy tobacco. A brilliant idea never strikes a donkey."

The King was pleased with the humour but not with the truth of the remark, for the cap fitted him rather well.

THE JESTER, A WEATHERCOCK

THE Emperor Akbar was once taking a walk in his gardens, Birbal being at his heels, as usual.

Seeing some brinjals of white colour Akbar exclaimed: "Are they not beautiful? I love white brinjals."

"They are really beautiful, your Majesty," readily responded Birbal. "They are decidedly the loveliest vegetables I have ever seen. They are lovely to look at, lovely to touch and simply delicious to eat. You can eat them baked, boiled, fried and toasted—in soup, with meat, as a vegetable, with pudding, with dessert—in fact, in whatsoever way you like and with whatsoever dish. They will always come out delightful to taste. I can never praise them enough, Your Majesty. They are the best thing for the stomach, the best for the liver, and for the spleen, the best for the bowels, the best for the kidney, the best for the blood, the best for the brain, and the very best for the marrow and muscles. They can be taken in any state of health or illness, and they will always prove to be the best for the bile, the best for the phlegm, and the best for hot temperament. O! I love the white brinjals, I simply adore them."

Akbar was not carried away by these wild outbursts of "*bests*." He silently walked on till he came to another part of the garden. Then pointing to a brinjal of violet colour, he said: "Look, Birbal, are not the violet brinjals lovely? I like them better than the white ones, for they have less seeds and are not so phlegmatic in effect."

"Your Majesty," responded Birbal, "can there be better things than the violet brinjals? They are infinitely better than the white ones, which are simply uneatable on account of the seeds and productive of the worst phlegm. I would never allow them to be brought near the royal table nor would I allow them a place in the kitchen-garden. But the violet brinjals, O, I simply worship! They are the very best, prettiest, loveliest, sweetest, daintiest, tastiest—— "

"Stop your stupid 'ests,' you villain," cried Akbar. "How can you say contradictory things in almost the same breath, you vile weathercock? It is not the brinjals that you are praising. Your sole object is to flatter me by turning your panegyrics this or that way as you think I am favourably inclined."

Birbal was not to be squashed by this sudden and serious reproach. He boldly looked the Emperor in the face and said:—

"May it please Your Majesty to answer me: Am I the servant of Your Majesty or of those wretched brinjals?"

"SAVED BY A READY WIT"

BIRBAL, the court-jester of a Mahommedan Emperor, was a Brahman. He, by virtue of his wits and learning, often befooled some of the *Ulema* (Mahommedan learned men) attached to the Emperor's Court. So these *Ulema* were always seeking to pay him back in his own coin by exposing some point of his ignorance.

One day an earthquake shook the Capital of the Emperor, and the Monarch was eager to know the cause of the strange phenomenon. So the council of learned men were summoned and called upon to account for it. Now the *Ulema* found an opportunity to make Birbal confess for once that he was ignorant. So they said :—

"Your Majesty should put the question to Birbal. He boasts of his knowledge of the stars and taunts us with our ignorance of things so far off. Now, let him come forward with an explanation for the quaking of the earth on which he lives. We are quite sure he will not be able to give it and forget his brag that he knows all."

Birbal thought for a second and then said :—

"Your Majesty, we Pandits are burnt after death and our souls ascend up to heaven with the smoke of the body. So we are expected to have a knowledge of the sky. But the *Ulema* are buried in earth after death and so it is their

ONE OF THE ULEMA.

province to explain what goes wrong inside the bowels of the earth to cause this disturbance; the province is not mine."

WHY THE PALMS OF OUR HANDS ARE HAIRLESS

ONE day it struck the Badshah of Delhi as curious that the palms of his hands had no hair on them. Being at a loss to account for this he asked Birbal (the Court jester): "Why is it that the palms of my hands are without any hair?"

"Protector of Dependents,"* said Birbal, "how can hair grow on the lotus-hands of Your Majesty if they get no rest in giving away gold."

The Badshah said, "That may be the case with me, but what has rubbed off the hair of your palms?"

"Supreme Lord,"† replied the jester, "Your Majesty gives and your slaves receive. The gold flows from your hands into ours and so the friction is alike on both."

The Badshah was pleased with the witty reply, but at once bethought himself of another question to outwit his clown. "Well, there are many," he said, "who do not receive any gold. What do you say of their palms?"

Birbal sprang to his feet and after repeated salaams said: "King of Kings.‡ There is hardly any man that is not blessed with your Majesty's bounty. If there be any such, he must have been wringing his hands in disappointment."

Gold actually flowed from the Badshah's hands into Birbal's.

* Bande-Parwar. † Huzur-e-álá. ‡ Sháh-en-Sháh.

PISR-E-KHUDA
(Son of God)

A CLEVER man of some pretensions sought the presence of a Mahommedan King for a long time but was always refused access. He then had recourse to a strange way of announcing himself. Dressing himself in a fantastic garb and mounting upon a jaded horse, he rode up to the Palace-gate and demanded an interview with the King saying: "The *Pisr-e-Khuda* (son of God) has come down and would condescend to see the King."

This announcement was too bold not to be attended to and the King felt curious to see the impostor who claimed to be the Son of God. So he ordered the man to be shown in; and when he was ushered in, the King said :—

"Well, you claim to be the Son of God! Can you show me the Heaven and the path that leads to it?"

The pretender said after a moment's thought:

"Well, that is not my province. When I was sent down by my Father, I was told to look to matters relating to this earth, and not to Heaven which He reserves for Himself. So if you want to see the earth I can show it to you, and can also show you the path to your grave."

The King was pleased with the man's ready wit and appointed him one of his courtiers.

"PISR-E-KHUDA"

WHY DO JACKALS CRY ?

ONCE upon a time there was a King in India who was very foolish. He wondered why the jackals howled so lustily from time to time in a neighbouring jungle. One winter evening, when chill winds were blowing, the jackals raised their chorus—hundreds of them yelling out: "Huk-a-hoo-hoo-hoo." The King, unable to suppress his curiosity, asked one of his courtiers: "Why are the animals crying so bitterly ?"

"Protector of the poor,"* answered the courtier, "they are shivering with cold."

"What do they want then ?" asked the King.

"Shelter of the World,† they want comfortable houses and warm clothes."

The King, moved by the distress of the jackals, ordered the courtier to take from his treasury five hundred gold mohurs in order to build houses for the poor animals, and supply them with beds and blankets.

The wily courtier drew the amount and pocketed it—paying, of course, his fellow-sycophants their due share.

Days passed by without any mention of the

* *Garib-newáj.*
† *Jahán-panah.*

affair, till one night the jackals raised another chorus of loud complaints. The King at once sent for the courtier and asked :—

" Have you not yet attended to the wants of these poor complainants ? "

" Yes, Lord of the World,"* was the reply.

" Then why are they crying again ? " questioned the King.

" It is because they are satisfied, and are blessing Your Majesty with all their hearts."

" Oh ! really ! " rejoined the King, delighted with his splendid act of charity.

* *Prithwi-ndlh.*

A LOVERS' QUARREL

In a fight between two goats,
A funeral of a sage,
An overcast morning sky,
And quarrel between lovers,
The beginning is pompous
But in little action it ends.
(A Sanskrit verse).

A YOUNG married couple lived happily together. The husband loved the wife and the wife the husband. They had petty quarrels from time to time, but they soon made up their differences. One day it happened that they were both in a mood to quarrel seriously with anybody. The wife suspected that the husband did not love her as before; and the husband was worried over the loss of some money, of which he had never told his wife. So she was in a sour temper ready to vent it on him for nothing; and he was so low-spirited that he would do anything to avoid being vexed. "So now," started she, "you are sick of me, eh? I asked for some embroidered lace for my dress. You would not even speak a word!"

He: "For God's sake leave me alone; will you?"

She: "Leave you alone? Has it come to this? I left my father, I left my mother, and I left all my relations for you and you alone! and now——"

He: "You left your father, you left your mother—well, what is that to me? You always throw that in my teeth! I am quite fed up with it. Didn't *I* leave my father and leave my mother, in order to live with you—which no dutiful son* should do?—"

She: "So you've let the cat out of the bag! you are sorry for what you have done? Please do go back to your father and mother, as behoves 'a dutiful son.' Fate will take care of me. I will not live under the control of a mother-in-law nor will I slave away for your brothers and sisters in a joint family. I will never never do it, even if you cut me to pieces!"

Thus words led on to words, till at last the husband lost his patience and walked away, saying:—

"I won't swallow your reproaches any more. I have been a henpecked husband and a woman has lorded it over me. So I am going to give up the world—wife and all. To-day I become a *Yogi* never to return home to see you humpy, grumpy and down in the dumps. I'm sick of it all."

The wife had also become infuriated and she too left the house, saying in the hearing of her husband, "Don't you fancy that I shall go down

* In an Indian family father and mother are regarded more than wife. A dutiful son does not leave parents when he is married; but he and his wife both live with them, studying their comforts and happiness more than their own.

on my knees to implore you to stay at home. If you are going to leave me I know how to look after myself. I will go and earn my living by selling vegetables and fruit."

So they parted, and so they resolved not to

" THEIR EYES MET "

have anything to do with each other as long as they lived. He took up the gear of a *Sádhu*,* and she bought some vegetables and fruit to take round for sale.

The new *Sádhu* had to come to the village

* Ascetic.

to beg and the new vegetable-girl had to go round to sell her vegetables. In his heart of hearts the *Sádhu* wished that he might meet his wife, and the vegetable-girl wished she might meet her husband, each being eager to show the other the transformation.

The eventide had not fallen before two cries :—*" *Alakh*," " Vegetables wanted ? "—were heard simultaneously at a meeting of two paths and two figures stood facing each other. It was the transformed husband and wife. Their eyes met, and spoke a different language from what their tongues had uttered in the morning. Down dropped the begging bowl from his hand and the basket slid down from her head ; and he and she were locked in a loving embrace.

At nightfall the couple were back at the same house in the same happiness of old old love.

* Sans. *Alakshya* (Undefinable, *i.e.*, God), uttered by mendicants of a certain order.

EASILY PLEASED

MANY, many years ago, a Cabuli (inhabitant of Cabul) came to India. He was walking about in a town when some sweets in a confectioner's shop attracted his attention. He knew but a word or two of Hindustani. So without speaking a word he went up to an assortment of sweets and pointed them out with his finger. The confectioner, thinking that he wanted to know the name only said "khájá." Now this word means "sweets" as well as "eat up." The Cabuli knew it in the latter sense, and at once fell upon the *khájás* and quickly gormandised the contents of a big vessel. The confectioner demanded the price of them; but the Cabuli, not understanding him, walked away. The confectioner made a complaint to the Kotowal (Police Officer). The Kotowal ordered that the Cabuli should be seized, his hair shaved and his head besmeared with tar; then he should be mounted on a donkey and driven out of the town with the beating of drums, in order to declare that any man acting in such an unlawful way should be punished in the same manner. This punishment is really considered very humiliating in India, but the Cabuli seemed to take it with very good cheer, and felt rather honoured.

When he returned to his country many people asked him : " How did you like Hindustan ? "

He answered :—

" Oh ! a charming country ! You get all for nothing there. You go and point out a particular kind of sweetmeat and you are at once told to eat it . The police will come and honour you *gratis*. You get a shave for nothing, a hair-dye for nothing, a donkey to ride and music to accompany you—all for nothing.* Beautiful country ! Excellent country ! ! "

* *Muftmen Khájá, muftmen bajá*
Muftmen Khar, muftmen hazá (*m*)

WHO IS DROWNED?

ONE day, some girls were bathing in a stream. They were seven in number; but when they counted themselves after the bathe one was found to be missing. So they all began to cry. Some women were passing by, and on being told that one of the girls had been drowned, they too began to cry. People came running from all sides, and hearing of the sad accident they also began to cry. The loud wailing went on for some time and attracted the attention of some officers who obtained divers and fishermen to search for the dead body. Nets were drawn up and down the river, but the corpse of the drowned girl was nowhere to be found. So the attempt was given up and an officer sat down to write particulars of the accident; but the girls could not say which of them was drowned.

Said one of them: "We were seven in all, but when we count we find only six. I cannot say which of us is drowned."

Saying this the girl counted up the six and omitted herself.

"Then," said the officer, "I must write that you are drowned, for you are not counting yourself.

"In that case," said another girl, "we are all drowned, for we all counted, but none counted herself," and saying this she darted away with wild shrieks of laughter followed by her playmates.

THE BLACK DOG IS DEAD

A GENTLEMAN, who lived in a country house, had to come to town and stay there for some time. One day he was surprised to meet a servant of his in town, and being very anxious to know about his people he asked: " How are all my people ? "

" All well, Master," said the servant. " The *Kálá Kuttá* (black dog) is dead."

" Poor dog, how did it die ? "

" How could it live when it ate up the flesh of all the dead horses in the stable ? "

" Are the horses dead too ? What was the cause of their death ? "

" How could it be possible for them to live when there were no grooms to feed them ? "

" What became of the grooms ? "

" That which usually comes to people who get no food, having no one to give them their pay."

" Why were they not paid ? What became of the steward ? "

" How could he live when there was no cook to prepare his food ? "

A few questions more gave the gentleman to understand that all his people, with the exception of the servant, had died—a surprise for which he was not prepared by the news of the Kálá Kuttá's death.

A STRANGE CURE

THERE was a physician who was very skilful. His medicine seldom failed in its effect; and the effect was everlasting. For, after his treatment the soul of his patient would leave the body for good, never again to be attacked by any disease.

A poor man had an only son who fell ill. The physician was called upon to treat him, but for the first day he was not so successful as usual. The father complained that the boy had excessive palpitation of the heart, which must be stopped. The physician gave some medicine and promised to come next morning to see the effect. When he came, the first thing he did was to examine the boy and then he cried out in triumph: "Look here, the palpitation has stopped." The anxious father felt the inert body of the boy and cried out in despair, "But he is cold and stiff and does not move?"

"What of that?" said the physician. "Is not the palpitation gone?"*

Not heeding the physician the poor father and two of his relatives shook the boy to see if there was life in him. But it was extinct, freed from the frame of flesh and bones by the physician's efficient treatment.

* "Dhug dhugi to mit gayi."

Now, while the father was lamenting over the death of his son, his relatives were making arrangements for the burning of the dead body.

There were only three men and four at least were required to carry the bier. So they compelled the physician to aid them in carrying the corpse to the crematorium.

Some time after, the same physician had a call to attend a sick man. He would not go unless he had a guarantee to find four men ready at the house of the patient. The men, who came to take him, wondered why he imposed that condition and asked what he required the four men for. He said :—

" Aray Bhai,* it is an unpleasant business to carry dead bodies and I am never going to do it again. So I have made it a rule not to go to the house of a patient who cannot shew me beforehand four persons ready to carry his dead body to be burnt."

* Brother mine !

A PATENT CURE

THERE was a Viadya (Physician) who tried to have his son Haridas trained up in his profession. But the son was such an idiot that he could learn nothing of the lore of Hindu medicine. The poor father was hopeless of his son's future ; and, while on his death-bed, he said :

"Haridas, in spite of my best efforts I have not been able to make you learn anything of our hereditary profession. But I give you one secret which will enable you to keep up the appearance of a physician. Administer powdered Kalimirchi (pepper)* to anybody who comes to you for relief." Of course, Haridas could remember this much, and applied *Kalimirchi* to any case of disease that came up to him for treatment after his father's death.

One day an old woman came to him and asked for some medicine that would enable her to find her lost cow. Haridas at once gave her a big dose of *Kalimirchi*. The poor woman had no rest that night and she had to come out of her cottage to cool herself in the open air. In the small hours of the morning she found her cow grazing in a bush not far off from the house. The cow, being set at liberty, had gone out grazing into a distant jungle and had come

* In another version it is Haritaki.

back of her own accord. But the woman thought it was the effect of the medicine and cried out in ecstasy arousing her neighbours.

Thus Haridas was proclaimed far and wide as a wonderful physician, whose medicine had the effect of restoring even lost cows.

Soon after this incident the Raja of the country sent for Haridas. His territory was going to be invaded by an enemy and he had not sufficient forces to oppose him ; so he asked Haridas to prescribe some medicine to defeat the enemy. Haridas at once prescribed *Kalimirchi*. An enormous quantity of *Kalimirchi* was therefore accumulated and powdered. Then the powder was mixed with flour which was sent to the grocer of the frontier to be supplied to the enemy's camp—as the flour of the best quality. The medicine was sure in its effect, for when the officers and many soldiers of the invading army had eaten bread made of this flour they felt as if they had been poisoned ; and thus put about, they beat a hasty retreat.

Then was Haridas installed in world-wide Fame !

ADVENTURES OF OPIUM-EATERS

I

THERE was a man who ate so much opium that his brain became quite muddled. He did not sleep but dozed day and night, and was haunted by dreams and fancies.

One night he forgot to latch the door of his cottage, and while he was dozing and dreaming, a thief stole in and ran away with one of his brass pitchers.

The opium-eater felt very crestfallen at finding himself thus robbed, for he had always boasted of his being wide awake day and night. He therefore made up his mind to tempt the thief in again and then catch him. So the next night he kept his door ajar and placed another pitcher near it.

The thief was jolly glad to find himself invited to steal away another pitcher. When the opium-eater discovered that he was twice robbed he could not contain his rage. He tried the same plan on the following night, but with the same result.

Thus baffled once and again in his attempt to catch the thief, the opium-eater lashed himself into a fury. He swore by many names that a common thief should not overreach a man of his skill and caution, and he devised such a plan as would outdo any thief, namely, to place *himself* at the very spot from which his pitchers were stolen. Thus, at night, he took the place of his pitcher and waited for the thief. He fancied himself to be a vessel, being sure that the thief would take him as such and play into his hands, to be seized and brought to book.

The thief, who had the pleasure of being presented with a pitcher every night, came at his usual hour. But great was his surprise to find the opium-eater sitting near the door with his hands and feet tucked in and dozing away. He stamped his feet and coughed aloud ; but that did not arouse the opium-eater, who still lay silent and motionless. Then he picked up a pebble and threw it at him. "*Tun-n,*" said the opium-eater imitating the sound of a metal vessel as well as he could. Thereupon the thief took a bamboo rod and gave him a push with it. "*Bub-bub-bub,*" bubbled the opium-eater, feigning that water was flowing out of himself, the supposed pitcher.

The thief could now understand the meaning, and without waiting to enjoy the fun any longer, he gave him a sound kick and ran away. The opium-eater poured out his "Bub-bub-bub" till he fell dozing again. When in the morning he was aroused by his neighbours, he sprang to his feet and cried out : "Defeated ! the cursed thief is defeated ! He did not make bold to carry me away. Oh, had he but once lifted me I should have held him in a vicelike grip till he was put in the lock-up."

II

An opium-eater ran through his wealth and was becoming poorer and poorer day by day.

His wife was very anxious that he should go out in search of employment, and save the family from utter ruin by earning some money. She daily admonished him, till at length the opium-eater was aroused to understand the state of affairs.

"Let me have my bag and umbrella," he said. "I shall leave this very day in search of employment—never to return till I have made money. You will see how active I can be, and what is my worth! In a few months hence you will roll in wealth—in gold and silver, I say."

"Don't blow your own trumpet," said the wife. "Empty vessels sound much. Deeds are better than words, so you had better prove your words by deeds."

Saying this she gave him his bag and umbrella, and he left the house. He had not gone far away from his village when he sat down to rest. and presently fell into a doze. Night had fallen when he woke up, and seeing some light in the distance, he directed his steps towards it. He walked on till he reached a village, and seeing a big house not far off from him he went and knocked at the front door. When a woman, with a veil on, had answered the door, he begged for food and a bed for the night.

[You must remember that there are no hotels or inns in Indian villages. Strangers depend on the hospitality of the inhabitants.]

"My husband is not at home," said the woman, "and my children are asleep. I cannot, therefore, admit you."

The opium-eater was turning to go away, when on second thoughts the woman said to him :

" It would be a sin to refuse a man hospitality, so come in and rest here for the night."

The opium-eater was glad to follow the woman, who led him to a room and gave him water with which to wash his hands and feet. She then cooked some food and served it to her guest, who remarked :—

" How like my own house this one looks ! "

Then when the woman came to serve some more *Rotis** the opium-eater had a glimpse of her face under the veil, and remarked :—

" How like my wife this woman looks ! "

The woman gazed at him and suddenly exclaimed :—

" Oh, you old villain, did you not say that you would not return till you had earned vast wealth, and you come back in six hours ? "

It did not take the opium-eater long to perceive that after a day's journey he had arrived at the place whence he started.

III

An opium-eater was once returning home at midnight. In a lane he was challenged by a police constable who was going his round. To avoid being suspected as a thief, he quickly pressed close to a wall and stood up against it still and silent. The constable challenged thrice, but getting no response, went up to the dumb figure and asked many questions ; but there was no reply. Thinking the man was

* Chapatis or Indian loaves.

deaf too, he gave him a hard push with his baton. Then the opium-eater spoke out :—

"Have you not eyes to see that I am but a *picture* drawn on the wall?"

"Yes, I quite see that," replied the constable, "but I will not allow a picture to be hung up here in this lane. You must hang yourself in the Police Station, at least for this night."

IV

In a den of opium-smokers in Calcutta the body of a beheaded man was found by the police. On inquiry it transpired that the opium-smokers had held on the previous night a *Káli-pujá*.* There was a woman among them who stood as Káli on the breast of a man, representing Shiva. Another man was deemed to be a goat and he was sacrificed before the Káli. They then took the supposed Káli and Shiva and the head of the sacrificed man to the Ganges to be thrown into the waters [a ceremony which is called *bisarjan*, by which the spirit of the god or goddess is supposed to leave the image.] The man and woman, of course, swam out of the water ; and all went home.

Next day, when they were all hauled up before the police court, the woman was asked what had become of the head of the sacrificed man. She tried to refresh her memory and then answered:

"Yes, I remember now. That man used to come and used to smoke too. But I cannot call to mind if he had a head at all."

* Worship of the goddess Káli, who is shewn standing on the god Shiva.

THE LAZIEST MAN IN THE EMPIRE

I

ONCE the Emperor of Delhi wanted to know who was the laziest person in his empire. The police made active searches, and at last presented to His Majesty two men whom they described as the very laziest in the world.

"But," said the Emperor, "I want to know which is the lazier of the two."

The policemen submitted that it was impossible to make that distinction, and therefore they had brought both instead of one.

The Court-Jester, Birbal, interposed: "I'll suggest to you a method of making the distinction. Place both the men in a wooden house and set it on fire. There should be men ready to put out the fire as soon as our test is finished."

The Emperor approved the idea and Birbal's suggestion was acted upon.

Now, when the house was on fire, one of the two idlers, without trying to move from his bed only said:—

"Where shines the sun?"*

His mate replied: "Who would trouble to open his eyes?"†

* *Kahán ravi jalay*

† *Kaun ánkh Kholay*

The fire was extinguished and the second man was considered to be the fittest for the title "The Laziest Man in the Empire," as he was too lazy to open his eyes to see where the fire was burning.

II

While the police had been scouring the country in search of the laziest man, they tumbled upon two men lying under a date palm. On the cheek of one of them lay a ripe date which had fallen from the tree, and he stretched his tongue in vain to draw it into his mouth. When a policeman asked them who they were, this man said :—

"Eh, Bhaiya ! (brother) will you help me by putting this date into my mouth so that I may eat it ?"

"You lazy rascal !" said one of the policemen, and promptly kicked him.

The other man who was lying by muttered drowsily :

"Well done ! The rogue deserves punishment—he is so lazy ! A dog came and licked my lips—I told him to drive it away—he wouldn't. Give him a good thrashing—he is so lazy !"

Before the police complied with his request they bundled *him* away to their officer as a fit candidate for the distinction of the "Laziest Man in the Empire."

ULLU RAI

UNDER the overlordship of the Moghul Emperors, there ruled in a small state a very wise Raja whose son was a perfect simpleton, and was called Ullu Rai.

When on his death-bed, the Raja addressed his officials and courtiers and said, "I know my son is an utter fool, but I cannot die in peace unless I have your promise that you will be faithful to him in spite of his faults and failings."

All the officials and courtiers cried out with one voice — "Ghanikhamá Annadátá (Great Mercy, oh giver of food!) Have we eaten your salt so long as to be unfaithful to your Heir Apparent? We will die rather than allow a hair of his to be touched."

The Raja died and Ullu Rai was installed in his place. It was not long before he became a nuisance to the whole state. He turned out the old trusted officials and filled their places with unworthy men. These bad men worried the honest citizens and maltreated all.

One day they said to Ullu Rai: "Garib newáj (Protector of the poor), why do you not keep an eye on the movements of the ex-minister? He is trying to overthrow us."

Ullu Rai remembered the warning, and in the evening when the citizens with the ex-minister came to pay their respects to him he cried out:—

"Look at my eyes. I am keeping one of them on each and every movement of the ex-minister's limbs; and before he makes the slightest move to capsize any of my new men I shall turn him upside down."

With these words he was going to trip up the

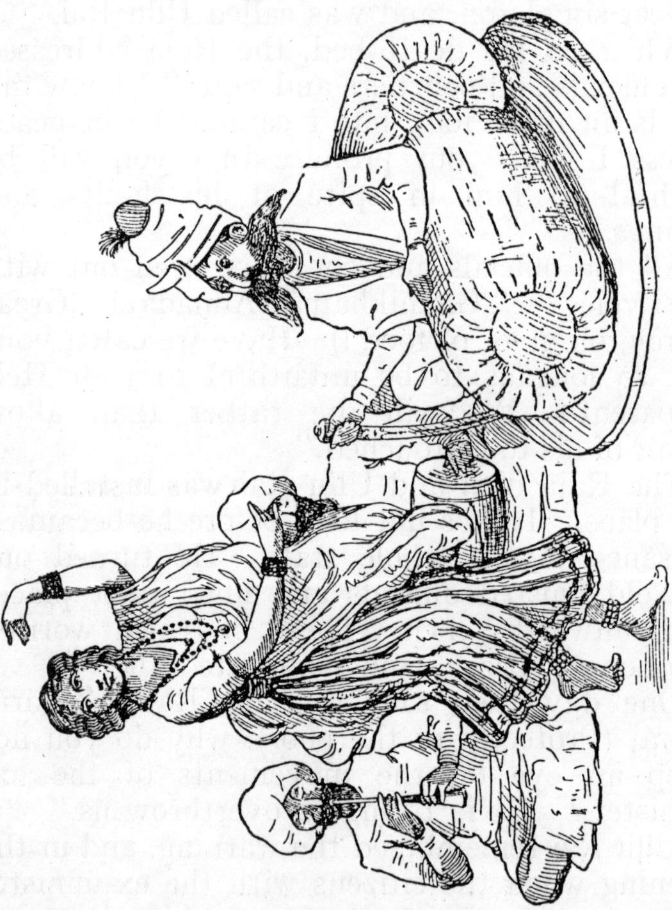

ULLU RAI.

poor old man in one of his sleights of wrestling, when he was checked.

Insults like this and oppressions by the new officials of no birth or breeding filled the land with discontent and people clamoured for justice. Complaints after complaints were sent up to the Moghul Emperor, who at last decided to depose the unfit ruler. But before taking steps he deputed one of his Wazirs to make sure if Ullu Rai was really as big a fool as reported.

News of the Emperor's intention reached Ullu Rai and his people. The Wazir was due at his capital in a day or two and he did not know what to do. The ex-minister, who had pledged his word of honour to the late Raja to help his son, now came forward and said :

" You need not fear at all, my lord. I will manage everything. Only do as I tell you. Dismiss all these unworthy rogues and call in the old officials—this is the first step you have to take."

Ullu Rai was ready to do anything to avoid deposition.

The old minister continued :—

" The second step is to learn from me how to receive the Wazir and how to talk with him. You must not allow the Wazir to ask you any question, but commit to memory the questions I dictate and put them to him one by one. Bear in mind that you are to stop speaking the moment I give the signal for it by pulling a rope, one end of which will be tied to the girdle of your trousers and the other will be in my hand in the adjoining room."

These instructions were followed to the letter. Rehearsals were held day and night till Ullu Rai learnt how to receive the Wazir, how to address him, and how to carry himself. He also learnt by rote the questions he had to put to the Wazir with polite accents avoiding his customary colloquialisms. The arrangement of the rope was, of course, not forgotten.

On the Wazir's arrival the programme was carried thrcugh safely and the rôle was faithfully played.

Question after question was put to the Wazir, such as " What are the favourite pursuits of the Emperor ? " " What are his Revenue arrangements ? " " How does he administer justice ? " and so on. The Wazir was quite charmed with the manners of Ullu Rai and at once thought that the reports against him were baseless.

At last Ullu Rai came to his tether's end when his questions were finished. To keep up the conversation he had to say something. So he ventured a question of his own, " Do they try to turn you upside down ? "

This he said in his characteristic slang quite unintelligible to the Wazir, who had to say, " I beg your pardon ? "

But in the meantime there was a hard pull at the rope. " I beg your pardon ? " repeated the Wazir.

Ullu Rai only said " *Ab to khinch gayi* " which implied : " (I must stop) now that (the rope) has been pulled." It might also mean, " I am strung up." The Wazir took it in the latter sense and as a signal to end the conversation. So he took his leave and spoke very highly of Ullu Rai to the Emperor, mentioning that his inability to understand one question only made Ullu Rai end the conversation abruptly.

"THE MIGHTY SPEAR"

THERE was a Raja who was not very clever. His ministers could dupe him as they liked.

One day the Raja was insulted by the chief of a neighbouring State. He flew into a rage and said to his Chief Minister :—

"Our neighbour has sent me an insulting message. I must punish him for it, so make preparations for war. . . . But wait, he is very powerful. Can you not think of some device ?"

The Minister thought for a little while and then said, "Yes, your Majesty, I have thought of a device. We could make a spear 100 miles long so that *it baithe ut máre* (sitting here we may strike there)."

The Raja said, "Excellent idea ! Go, have the spear made without any delay."

"But," said the Minister, "it will cost much. The spear must be made wholly of steel in order to pierce all the enemy's soldiers."

"So much the better. What do you think it will cost ? Will half a million rupees suffice ?"

"Quite enough, your Majesty," replied the Minister.

"Take the amount from my treasury and hurry up. But everything must be done with the strictest secrecy."

The Minister took the money, but all that he did was to fill up his private chest with the strictest secrecy. He, however, employed some of his servants to keep hammering on an anvil so that the Raja could hear the din.

A few days passed and the Raja, impatient to have his revenge on the neighbouring chief, asked his Minister :—

" Is the spear ready ? "

" It is nearly ready, Sire," answered the Minister, " but I fear one thing."

" What is that ? " asked the Raja.

" I fear very much the chance of the enemy's snatching away the spear and using it against us. The case would then be reversed—*Ut baithe it mare* (sitting there, strike here). Then we shall all be killed."

" Quite possible, quite possible ! " cried the Raja. " Break the spear then into pieces. You must make haste lest it should fall into the hands of the enemy."

" But it would be a tremendous task to break the huge spear of solid steel into pieces. The cost would be about as much as it has been to make it. And then all that steel has to be removed away from the enemy's reach, and the mouths of the smiths have to be gagged."

" Yes, yes, I see ! " cried the Raja. " But it has to be done at any cost. Don't you see the risk of delay ? Then take another half million from my treasury and split up the spear as soon as possible."

So a million rupees passed safely into the Minister's private chest. The Raja could hear the din of hammering on the imaginary spear and the reports that the work of splitting it up was in full swing.

A CLEVER BROKER FINDS HIS MATCH

IN India, betrothals are generally made by match-makers. They try to hush up the defects of the boy or the girl going to be married. So a clever match-maker managed to arrange the marriage of a blind girl with a handsome boy. The trick he played had been to show the girl under a veil to the boy's guardians, and when pressed to take off the veil he had it raised to the eyes only. He said that the girl was so bashful that she would not anyhow allow her veil to be completely taken off. Now, bashfulness in a girl was reckoned as a merit, and the boy's party consented to the marriage without any further examination. So the wedding came off and when the priest had finished his rites in uniting the couple, the bride's match-maker cried out :—

"The bride—my blind client—has scored a success."*

The bridegroom's match-maker retorted, "I'll admit it, when my client stands up!"† He meant that the success could be judged if his client would stand up.

This made the bride's party request the bride-

* "Jag jit lino meri Káni."
† Var thand ho to jáni.

groom to stand up unsupported by others. But he could not, as he was lame. Then the match-makers of both sides looked full at each other

A RATH
A BULLOCK CHARIOT TO CARRY ZENANA LADIES.

with a wicked twinkling in their eyes in recognition of the fact that the one was a match for the other.

EMPTY VESSELS MAKE THE MOST SOUND

A BRAHMAN and his wife were reduced to abject poverty. They had no means to keep the body and soul together, and the insults of proud neighbouring women drove the Brahman's wife simply mad. She cruelly reproached her husband for not being able to remove his poverty, the sting of which she could bear no longer. The Brahman took his wife's admonition to heart and silently walked away. When he had gone a long way off from the village he sat down to rest under the shade of a tree. He was all but dead with hunger and fatigue and was going to say his last prayers. Just then a god in the form of a mendicant came to him and gave him a *shankha* (conch-shell), saying :—

"Take this conch-shell, O poor Brahman. It will give you such little money as you ask it for, in order to meet only your daily wants."

Saying this the mendicant vanished. The Brahman was jolly glad to get a godsend to remove his poverty. It was midday and he had not the strength left to walk back home. So he went to the landlord of the nearest village and asked for his hospitality. The landlord received him well and gave him provisions to cook for his meal. As the Brahman had to go to the river to bathe he left the conch-shell in his host's custody explaining its importance and magical properties. While the Brahman was away bathing the landlord tested the power of the shell by asking for some money which was forthwith given. He was too greedy to part with such a precious money-making instrument. So, when after having finished his meal the Brahman asked leave to go and to have his conch-shell back, the mean landlord denied all knowledge of such a thing being entrusted to his keeping, and turned away the Brahman as an impudent liar.

Dazed by this fresh stroke of adversity and smarting under the landlord's dishonest trick the poor Brahman came back to the spot where he had met the mendicant and bitterly lamented his lot. He passed the whole night under the tree. Early in the morning he got up and sat still with downcast eyes, reflecting on his sad career. Looking up, his eyes caught those of the same mendicant who had met him before and who was standing before him. He at once went on his knees and prayed for some fresh favour to save him from sure death. The mendicant consoled him and gave him another conch-shell with instructions that he should go back to the same landlord and refuse to give him the second shell until he had returned the first.

"This shell," the mendicant rejoined, "has greater magical powers of which you need not avail yourself. You may tell the landlord to ask it for any amount."

With these words the mendicant vanished, and the Brahman acted on his instructions. The landlord was very glad to see the Brahman with another conch-shell, accredited with greater magical powers. As desired by the Brahman he at once asked the shell to give him one thousand rupees.

"One thousand rupees?—too small an amount! Ask for more"—was the prompt answer of the shell.

The landlord's heart gave a bound to hear this big offer. He begged the Brahman to sell him the shell. Otherwise he threatened to take it by force. The Brahman said:—

"I want no price. Give me back my first shell and this is yours."

The exchange was immediately made and the Brahman made haste to march home with his first shell. The landlord was impatient to see a room filled up with coins. So he ordered one of his rooms to be emptied and whitewashed. When the room was ready he took the shell and placing it on a platform, said:—

"Now conch-shell, you said that one thousand rupees were too paltry an amount. Then come forth, give me one *lákh** of rupees."

"One lákh? Too small, ask for more," promptly answered the shell.

"Oh! then give me a crore (ten million) rupees," demanded the landlord.

"One crore? Too small, ask for more," was the ready response of the shell.

The landlord went on naming a larger and

* 100,000.

larger amount *ad infinitum,* till he was at his tether's end. But to each of his demands the same answer was given—viz.: "Too small, ask for more."

At last the landlord despaired and found out that he was too avaricious to get anything, and the conch-shell was only promissory and nothing else. He named it "Gapore* Shankh," *i.e.*, a conch-shell which only makes big offers and pays nothing.

Thenceforth a man with empty talks and promises, is called a "Gapore Shankh" or "Lápar† Shankh."

[There is another story current in which the first gift to the Brahman is said to be a pot, supplying sweets inexhaustively: the second a pot containing a rope and hammer to bind and belabour any person who would open it.]

* Given to tall talks—pronounced as *Gaporde.*
† False.

BARÁ BHAIYA'S LETTER*

AT a shop in one of the streets of Bombay a Marwari boy was found weeping. All the Marwari † merchants of the neighbourhood flocked around him and asked him the cause of his grief. The boy flung a letter at them pointing to a line which ran as follows: "*Chacháji Aj mar gayá*" (Uncle, to-day, has died).

The meaning of the writer was:—"Uncle has gone to Ajmer." But as *Ajmer* was written as *Aj* (to-day) *mar* (die), the sentence meant: Chachaji (uncle) died to-day.

The letter was dated five days ago. So one of the Marwaris said:—

"How can this be possible? This letter is dated the 3rd instant and we saw your uncle at the railway station of Nasik only yesterday, the 7th. There can be no mistake about it, for my friends Jowanmal and Kalyanmal were with me. They will bear me out when I say that we saw him in flesh and blood only yesterday and said *Jai Shri-Krishna* (glory to Shri-Krishna,—a form of salutation) to him and that

*This literally means a letter from an elder brother. But it also signifies a Gospel handed down by some high authority whose veracity cannot be called into question.

† Of Marwar, Rajputana.

he said he was on a pilgrimage going from shrine to shrine."

Another man said :—

" Did you not get a *tár* (telegram) from your uncle only yesterday ? I read it out to you. He said in it that he arrived at Nasik *via* Pushkar (a shrine near Ajmer) and Abuji (Mount Abu). Then how could he die on the 3rd ? "

The boy thought for a while and then replied :

" What you say is all very true. But this letter comes from *Bará Bháiyá* (elder brother) who cannot write what is false."

* * *

There are many absurd things in this world which are believed because they come down from " Bará Bháiyás."

A FATAL BELIEF IN LUCK

A RAJA'S son and a poor grocer's son were born on the same day and at the same hour. The grocer, of course, had faith in the influence of stars and consoled himself with the belief that the new-born prince and his babe would have the same fate in life. So for twice ten years he waited to see some eventful turn in the prince's life—which, he was sure would befall his son also.

At his twentieth year the prince went out hunting and was successful in bagging many animals. While returning he strayed into the Himalayan kingdom of a Raja who received him cordially and gave him in marriage his only daughter—a princess of matchless beauty whom the prince had already met romantically in the woods near her palace.

When the prince came home with his trophies of the hunt, his handsome wife and immense wealth in the shape of a wedding dowry, the grocer was animated with the desire of sending his son out hunting in the belief that he would meet with the same good fortune. So, he equipped him with a rusty spear he had in his house and gave him a hearty send-off assuring him of the grand luck that was in store for him.

Now, the grocer's boy, who had never learnt how to hunt, was at a loss to decide where to go and what to do. He was roaming about in the forest aimlessly, till he found a big frog jumping away across his path. He at once gave chase and after a hard run just managed to catch hold of one of its legs, when he fell down into

HE CAUGHT A FROG

a pit and broke his legs. He could not rise, but held the frog fast and would not let it go.

The grocer was impatient to know what luck his son had achieved. So he followed in his track and finding him nowhere in the forest cried out at the top of his voice :

" Son, son—where are you, my dear ? "

" Here, father," answered the son from the distant pit.

"What have you got?"

"A frog, father."

"A frog?—let it go. Come follow up your hunt. You are sure to have a great fortune."

"I cannot come, father—my legs are broken."

The poor grocer hastened to the pit and was greatly moved to see his son with broken legs, but with the frog held fast in his hand. Then he said:—

"Poor me! A fool that I was to believe in Fate and harbour ambition." *Gain a frog and lose your legs.**

* Bengali saying: "*Ldbhey bang Apachaye thang.*

THE GIANT AND THE PIGMY

THERE was once a powerful giant who made a tour throughout India, declaring that any man who could give right answers to his questions by signs, should be richly rewarded by him, and those failing to answer them correctly should be put to death. Hundreds of men came forward to answer his questions with the object of winning the tempting reward, but they failed and met death at the hands of the unrelenting giant.

At last he entered the territory of a Raja who was very timid and wanted to get rid of him with presents and plausible words without producing any candidate for answering his questions. But a cowherd boy came up boldly and offered to face the giant's questioning. The Raja tried to dissuade the audacious boy from rushing into the mouth of what seemed to him to be sure death, but the boy stuck doggedly to his resolve. Eventually he was introduced to the giant as the only man in the Raja's territory who had ventured to come forth and answer his questions. So before a large assembly presided over by the Raja, the giant and the pigmy cowboy stood face to face. The giant showed one finger to the boy by way of questioning and the boy answered promptly by showing two fingers. Thereupon the giant stretched up both his arms towards the boy and then waved them towards the sky. The boy stretched his hands towards the earth and then gave a bound.

While all the horror-stricken people expected each second the end of the boy's life, the giant with a look of satisfaction directed his steps towards the Raja's seat.

The Raja was eager to know why he had spared the boy's life—which favour he had not extended to any other mortal; but at the same time he expressed his pleasure at seeing the poor boy treated so mercifully by him.

But the giant said: "On the contrary, he has won the prize I offered for right answers. You know, Raja, my questions were very hard, especially as they were put by signs. But the boy is very clever and he has succeeded where all others failed."

He then proceeded to explain to the Raja and his Council what the questions and answers were:

"I asked," he said, "by showing one finger, whether there is only one principle in nature. He answered by showing two fingers that there are two: *matter* and *spirit*.* I then asked him how it was that he did not fall off from the earth. He answered by signs which indicated that it was the attraction towards the centre of the earth that held him to it, and illustrated

* *Prakriti* and *Purusha*, as in the theory of Duality of Sánkhya.

it by taking a jump.* I am quite satisfied, and I leave with you this precious jewel to be given to him as my promised reward. I cannot wait and must leave at once."

When the giant had gone, the Raja called the boy, and before the whole assembly addressed him thus:

"Boy, I have the greatest pleasure in awarding you this precious reward left for you by the Giant. I am proud to think that my State has produced such a clever boy as you, who has had the wit and knowledge to answer questions which baffled the best intellects of all other States. But what I cannot understand is this: how could you have the genius to read his questions and whence did you have all this knowledge of science and philosophy to answer them?"

"Oh, Raja," the boy interposed, "it was very easy. With one finger he meant to say, 'I will pierce one of your eyes'—I with two fingers answered, 'If you pierce one eye of mine, I will pierce both the eyes you have in your head.' Then he showed by his hands that he would uplift me and hurl me into the air. I by signs showed that I would come down to the ground quite safe and bolt away."

* This is apparently a modern rendering. In the original the giant is said to have asked: "What upholds the earth?" The boy's answer is understood to be: "The Snake" (the huge mythological Snake, called the Endless). The giant makes the sign with his clenched fist, representing a round object, which the boy takes for a threatened blow. The boy's sign in answer is the raised thumb, which is supposed by the giant to represent a snake, but by which the boy means to say: "Tush! I defy your threat."

A LEARNED DUNCE

A PANDIT returned from Benares* with his head full of lore. He could cite any passage from any of the six philosophies, grammar and mythology. But he had very little common sense.

His wife was very glad to see him back after such a long time, and felt a great regard for the vast learning for which he had become famous. She was boiling some milk when the Pandit arrived and as there was no water with which he could wash his hands and feet, she said to him :

" Would you mind seeing that the milk does not boil over ? I am going to fetch some water for you from the well, and there is no other person here. I shan't be long."

The Pandit said " Yes " and remained in charge of the boiling milk. In a few minutes the milk began to boil over. The Pandit becoming alarmed fell to repeating all the *mantras* (prayers) he had learnt and *sutras* (aphorisms), but without avail. His wife came hurrying back and seeing that the milk was overflowing poured some water into it, and it at once settled down. The Pandit was taken aback by what seemed to him a miracle. So he began to pray to his wife in words like these :

" Thou must be a goddess who hast powers more than any of my *mantras* possess. Oh, thou goddess, I pray to thee."

The poor wife was nonplussed and said : " You are a learned fool."

* Seat of Sanskrit learning.

COMMON SENSE—AN OCCULT POWER

A PANDIT of Benares was known to fame for his wondrous learning. He had a younger brother, who was not at all well-read but had a good deal of practical experience and common sense.

This younger brother was proud of his elder and had great reverence for him. He was always devoted and dutiful, as a younger brother ought to be in an Indian family. The Pandit, too, was much attached to him and relied on him for everything in household affairs.

The Pandits of Benares are often invited by the rich Hindus in all parts of India to their religious rites or festivals, especially *Shráddhas* (funeral rites). They and the local Pandits hold what is called *Shástrárthas* or discussions on such topics as are of religious or philosophical importance. After the discussion is over they are honoured by the host with gifts (*vidáya*). On their way back they visit out-of-the way places, where they have good receptions as well as gifts for the display of their learning.

Once our Pandit, attended by his brother, was touring in the country on his return from a *Shástrártha*. They left a village about four o'clock in the morning and had a good long walk before they arrived at another by eight. Here they halted to have their bath, say their prayers, cook, and have their noon-meal. They chose a place near a well under a banyan tree on the outskirts of the village, where they laid down their kit and sat down for a little rest.* They had not long been resting when they heard that a rich Raja lived in the village. So the Pandit sent his brother to the Raja in order to announce his arrival. The Raja made an appointment to receive the Pandit and also sent him flour, rice, *dál*, clarified butter, salt, vegetables and faggots, etc., to cook his food with.†

After having his bath the Pandit performed his *pujá* (worship), donned a silk dress, marked his forehead with sacred signs, and went to see the Raja.

His brother, after a bath, said his prayers and then cleared a spot to lay his stove, which consisted of three stone-pieces. He made the flour into dough,‡ and lighting the fire he began to cook the vegetables.

On his arrival at the Palace the Pandit was asked by one of the courtiers the meaning of a word which was outside his vocabulary. This gave the courtiers an opportunity of jeering at the learning of a Pandit of Benares. The next question was put by the Raja himself, who said :

* The conservative Pandits of Benares may take snuff, but do not smoke. Other people sit down to smoke after a walk of a few miles and then resume journeying.

† Brahman Pandits do not take food unless cooked by near relatives or kinsmen ; so, when visiting places, they are not asked to dinner, but are given dry provisions that they may cook their own food.

‡ Dough is made first in order to give it time to soak well.

SOME TYPES OF INDIAN WOMEN

"I shall admit that you are a learned Pandit if you can read my thoughts."

The Pandit said: "I can answer any question you put to me from grammar, literature, philosophy, astronomy or the laws, but I have not studied the occult science of thought-reading which belongs only to the *Yogis*, who are rarely seen but in unapproachable caves in the mountains. We, Pandits, are not Yogis. We are only scholars. So the reading of your thoughts is quite beyond me."

This answer was greeted with loud laughter from the Raja and his courtiers, who had very little urbanity in them. The poor Pandit took offence at this, left the palace in disgust, and returned to his brother, who was waiting for him with the prepared meal.

The Pandit looked dreadfully cross and refused food. So the brother asked the cause and was told what had taken place at the palace.

"You had better attend to the food," said the brother, "and I will go and face the music. This does not seem to be a place for you, the people are evidently idiotic and only fit to be handled by an idiot like myself."

Saying this he donned a silk dress, marked his forehead, and went and announced himself to the Raja, giving himself the airs of a very great scholar. The Raja's court was still making a song of the victory over a Pandit of Benares; so they were looking forward to another exultation and readily received the new Pandit to make fun of him too.

As soon as the new-comer was seated, the courtier nearest him said :—

"Well, Pandit Maháraj, you hardly know what a learned court you have to deal with. Many a Pandit has come and gone, but none has answered my question. Can you tell me the meaning of the term : '*Ghánwarghoon*' ?"

The brother of our Pandit slapped the man promptly in the face and cried out as follows :—

"You dunce, you don't say the whole thing, no wonder the Pandits could not explain it. You should say :—

'*Agay churd-churd páchhay choon*
Tákay, páchhay ghánwar ghoon'*

(the sound made in milking cows in a pail, the first sound is '*churd churd*' ; second '*choon*' ; and the third '*ghánwar ghoon*')."

The whole court burst into praises at the new Pandit's cleverness, and the courtier who had for so long a time been puffed up with pride at the admiration of the villagers, in whose eyes he loomed much bigger than the Pandits of Benares, looked very crestfallen.

The Raja said :—

"You are really one of the greatest Pandits living ; for none has up to now vanquished my brilliant courtier. Now can you tell me what my thoughts are ?"

"Yes," answered the new Pandit, "I can ; but only on condition that you will acknowledge before the assembly whether I tell you the truth

* *Agay*—Before ; *páchhay*—after ; *tákay*—of that ; *tákay páchhay*—after that.

or not and pay me my honorarium at once if I succeed in reading your thoughts correctly."

"Certainly," answered the Raja, "I agree."

"Well, Raja," said the new Pandit, "the thought that is uppermost in your mind is that you wish good to all of your people and desire to see them prosperous. You want to lead a pious life and then to attain heaven. You wish that your son may be as brilliant as you, and also more prosperous. Now, tell me before all if I have not told you the truth?"

The Raja could not but say "yes." He had also to fulfil his promise to honour and reward the Pandit then and there.

When the brothers met, great was the astonishment of the real Pandit to learn how successful his unlettered brother had been where he, with all his knowledge and learning, had failed; and he was now convinced that it is not always learning that scores a victory.

FEMALE GOSSIP

ONCE upon a time a Pandit, returning home across a field, had a bad fit of coughing and expectorated on the ground. On looking down he found to his amazement a white feather sticking in what he had spat out. He pondered long to guess how it came there and at last arrived at the conclusion that it had come through his throat. A depressing thought took hold of him and he had no peace of mind until he could mention this extraordinary happening to his wife, pledging her to secrecy. His wife promised to tell nobody about it.

Presently a neighbouring lady called to see her and the first thing the wife said to her was: "My dear——, my mind is too full of one thing, but I promised my husband I would tell no one."

"Well," said the neighbour, "I don't pry into others' affairs, so it is best to keep the secret to yourself if you cannot believe in me. You know I am never nosy."

"But you see," said the Pandit's wife, "it bodes ill for my husband and I must have advice in this, so if you swear you will tell nobody I will confide in you."

"Have I ever repeated anything you have

confided to me? What do you think of me? Do you take me to be a gossip?"

"Oh no, oh no, I feel sure you will not repeat the secret. It is this:—When my husband was coming home he was seized with a bad fit of

SOME TYPES OF INDIAN WOMEN.

coughing, and what do you think, he spat out?—Lots of heron's feathers!"

"Good heavens!" exclaimed the neighbour, "whatever can be the cause? But you must keep this secret and not let people know, for they will spread this serious news all over the place."

Saying this the lady was eager to take her

departure, pretending she had some pressing business on hand.

Great was her anxiety, on running home, to come across a friend to whom she could confide the great secret welling up in her bosom. So to the first woman she met, she said :

" Will you promise not to tell anybody and I will tell you a great secret ? Our Pandit has coughed up a heron. What do you think of that ? "

" Coughed up a heron ? " exclaimed the friend, " is it possible ? How could he have had it in his stomach ? But rely on me, I'll tell no one."

Ere long another lady was put into possession of the news that live herons had come out through the Pandit's throat.

In an hour or two the whole village rang with the rumour that flights of herons were coming out of the Pandit. Thus he was besieged by the villagers who came to see the wonderful sight of flights of herons coming out of his throat.

People of other villages also got hold of the news which flew on the wind too fast in more and more exaggerated forms. They too came round in hundreds of thousands to see the unheard-of miracle.

The poor Pandit went off his head and had to run away and hide himself until the " nine days' wonder " passed away.

WHERE IGNORANCE IS NOT BLISS

A SANSKRIT drama was being played before a Raja and his people. In the course of the performance one of the players advised his stage-wife to have patience, by citing some verses meaning :—" The night has nearly worn to its close and the day is about to dawn. That being the case it is better to bide the short time and wait till the morn patiently "—and so on.

The Rajkumar (Raja's son) was so much struck with these lines that he gave away his shawl to the actor in reward. The Rajkumari (Princess) too took off her precious ring and sent it by her *Dasi* (maid) to the actor by way of showing her appreciation. Then up got the Mantri's (Prime Minister's) son. He went straight to where his father was seated and gave him a slap on the face. The Mantri hugged his son to his bosom and patted him on the back.

The Raja was greatly surprised to see all this. He put a stop to the performance and first asked his son to explain what made him wax so bounteous on such commonplace lines as those cited by the player. He replied :—

" Father, the lines in themselves might not have much value, but in relation to my particular case they are worth their weight in gold. I came of age long ago, but have not yet been entrusted with the government of the kingdom. So I intended to kill you this night, and declare myself as King. But the lines suggest that it is no good being impatient for anything which is

INDIAN MUSICAL INSTRUMENTS

A QUESTION OF ANTIDOTES

A MAN had an acre of land in which he used to grow corn. In harvest time his corn-field was devastated by insects, so he was obliged to breed frogs in the field to eat them up. In course of time the frogs grew so numerous that he could not enter the field without being molested by them. He therefore had to import some snakes to eat up the frogs. They again grew so many in number in a few years that the man had to give up cultivating the field. But the snakes did not keep to the field but gradually invaded his house, which was near by. Then one by one his whole family, including himself, fell victims to the poisonous bites of these venomous creatures.

A QUESTION OF HABIT

A WIDOW of a high family married a tanner. When she went to live with the poor tanner in his house, she was dreadfully upset by some bad smell. She at

THE CHARKHÁ
(AN INDIAN WOMAN SPINNING)

once betook herself to the task of thoroughly scouring and cleaning the house, and in a few days it became neat, clean and tidy. Then she said to her husband :—

"Look here, your house was simply stinking when I first came here. I could not bear the offensive smell that was in it. Now I have cleaned it so well that the smell is there no longer. It is ever so pleasant to live here now."

"Yes," replied the tanner, "to me the house always smelt as it does now. Clean it howsoever you like you cannot free it from the smell of hides and leather. The same smell is there that used to be. But it is only your nose that has made the difference. For it is now used to the smell."

OTHERS ERR, BUT NOT MYSELF

FOUR Mahommedans were offering prayers at a mosque. One by chance said something not belonging to the prayer. The man next to him cried out :—

" You fool, you have spoken out in the midst of your prayer. Therefore, all your prayer goes for nothing."

" And yours ? " cried out the third man, " you too have spoken, so your prayer cannot have any effect."

The fourth Mulla muttered to himself :— " They are all speaking. Thank God I am not."

A WEAK INTERMEDIATOR

ONCE upon a time in a forest in India a sparrow saw from its nest that a huge elephant was going to attack another, which was by appearance smaller and weaker than itself and was fleeing before it in fright.

Indignant at this atrocious attack on a weaker animal, the sparrow made up its mind to check the assailant by personal interference. So she took to wing and hovering around the head of the agressive elephant began to chirp, and to say:

"Stop, you oppressive animal. Is it not cowardly to attack one weaker than yourself and frightened at you? Is it not your place to protect it instead? It is against all law of "animality" to attack and oppress the weaker, and I certainly will not allow this outrage which is worse than brutal."

Louder and louder grew its chirpings as on and on came the pursuing elephant gaining upon the pursued. But as no notice was taken of its protests the sparrow was furious and chirped her loudest, as it were to say:—

"You big burly brute! You set at naught my good advice and kindly office of intermediation? I said I would not allow this and I mean it."

Just then the attacking elephant was falling upon the other. With wings outspread and beak wide open the sparrow flew between the two, as if to separate them by force. In a second the two mountains of flesh closed in upon it and squashed it to pulp The elephants had their fight out and afterwards became the best of friends ; but the poor little dicky-bird never came back to life or light again.

A STUPID WELL-WISHER

A RAJA had a trained monkey that was very sagacious. It danced attendance on the prince and did many things as well as a devoted servant could do.

One of the things it often did was to fan the prince when he was asleep on hot summer days.

Once when the prince was asleep, the monkey was fanning him in order to keep the air cool and also to ward off the flies from his body. [Flies are the worst pests of the Indian plains during summer days.]

One particular fly was causing very great annoyance to the monkey. When it was fanned away from one part of the prince's body it would swerve round and settle on another. It dodged and dodged and kept up this process until the monkey lost all patience.

Being resolved to kill the fly, which was then seeking to settle on the prince's breast, the monkey took the sword from under his pillow.*

Unsheathing the sharp blade and taking a good aim, it struck at the pertinacious fly. Down came the sword on the prince's breast and ran right through his heart. The fly flew away, but the poor prince struggled and groaned with agony till he died.

* The Rajas used to sleep with a sword in their bed, for the purpose of self-defence, if necessary.

ONE LAW FOR YOU—ANOTHER FOR ME

THE Brahman Pandits (learned priests) in India prescribe penances to people who come to them desiring to make atonement for sins which they may have committed.

Once a man sought the presence of a Pandit and asked:

"Maharaj,* what is the penance for the slaughter of a Makkar (spider)?"

"Spider? Spider-killing is a very great sin. The sinner will have to give away gold in charity. Eh?—let me see—one maund of grain and besides—you see—ghee (clarified butter)—and, and—cloths, five pieces, and—let me see—pujah (offerings) to Vishnu (Protector of the Universe)."

The Man: "I am so sorry you will be put to such heavy expenses."

The Pandit: "I? I? Why—why should I bear the expenses?"

The Man: "Because it is *your* son who has killed the *makkar.*"

The Pandit: "Eh! eh! my son? Let me see—I forgot—Oh! here it is in the *Shástras* (sacred books)!—I made a mistake; I did not see carefully—Makkar-killing needs *dokkar* (two *kowris*)†; so you see the penance is dokkar."

* Pandits are often addressed respectfully as 'Maharaj,' 'Maha'—great, 'raj'—kingdom. 'Maharaj'—one who has extensive sway. 'Maharajas' means great Kings.

† Kowris or shells were in India the exchange of the lowest value.

HINTS FOR THE WISE, AND FORCE FOR THE FOOLISH

DEGREES OF SELF-RESPECT.

THERE were four idle mouths who married the daughters of a rich man and lived on his income at his house.* At first they were treated with all consideration due to new sons-in-law. But soon the household domestics got tired of them and every day made some complaints.

As time went on the father-in-law felt the burden and the heavy expenses of keeping the four sons-in-law; and the mother-in-law too became sick of their constant quarrels with the servants and began to look upon them as regular nuisances. The couple held a consultation and decided to drop some hints to the sons-in-law to leave the house and earn their own livelihood.

Next day when the parasites were having their meal they were given no milk. They waited and waited, but no one came with the cups of milk, as was usual at the end of each meal.

* A rich man, blessed with many daughters, has sometimes to keep at his house quite a good number of sons-in-law. They are, in some cases numbered thus: Son-in-law No. I, No. II, etc.; and their rooms are sometimes called in fun "barracks."

The same disappointment was in store for them the following day, whereupon one of them said :

" My dear brothers, I smell a rat. It really cannot be a mistake ; it is surely an indication that we are no longer wanted here."

" Tush," said the others, it is not so serious as you imagine. They may be studying a little economy, and that's all. They cannot possibly want their dear and near sons-in-law to go away."

" You may try and kid yourselves," rejoined the first man, " with the belief that you are their dear and near relative. But to me the hint is enough. They have had too much of our dearness and nearness and they now want to be rid of us, the hangers-on. I am going to leave the house at once for good. If you are not disposed to do the same, you may please yourselves."

Saying this, he took leave of his comrades, picked up his things and left.

The others did not think it worth while to follow his lead. They rather laughed at his conduct and regarded him as being too thin-skinned.

The father-in-law was delighted with the partial success of his plan, and advised the cook to try it again.

Next day the three sons-in-law were deprived of the cakes that were usually served with their meals.

This was a sign serious enough for another son-in-law to take notice of.

He also passed the same remarks as the first man who had already gone, and bade adieu to the house.

The remaining two flatly refused to leave the house despite all the omissions in the courses for breakfast, dinner, and afternoon refreshment.*

At last the father-in-law instructed the cook to give them burnt food. This was too much for one of the remaining sons-in-law; and he departed in disgust.

The fourth, Dhananjaya by name, stuck to the house like a leech in spite of all insults. He pocketed them cheerfully and nothing could arouse his sense of indignation. He was quite dead to the feeling of self-respect.

Seeing that all his devices failed to make Dhananjaya leave the house, the father-in-law ordered his domestics to seize him by the neck and turn him out of the house, and in case he showed signs of resisting, to give him a good thrashing.

"Prahárena Dhananjayah" (Sanskrit).

Dhananjaya (goes) being thrashed.

* People in India generally take two regular meals, one about noon and another in the evening. Many of them take light refreshments in the morning and in the afternoon. The staple food is either rice or bread made of wheat.

A LAW UNTO HIMSELF

A GENTLEMAN was placed in charge of the Magistrate's office at a certain military station. A man was hauled up before him on a charge of murder.

The Magistrate asked the accused why

AN INDIAN COTTAGE.

he committed the murder. The murderer deposed :—

" Your Worship, I committed murder in a fit of anger. I was given grave provocation."

" You rascal," said the Magistrate, " don't you know it is a great crime to kill a human being ? I shall give you such a lesson that you will never think of murdering anybody in future. *Koi hai ?* " (Is there anybody ?)

" Hazir, Hurzar " (here at your service, my lord) cried a number of voices—chaprasis and constables.

" Pull this devil by the ears," ordered the Magistrate, " and make him sit down and stand up one hundred times and then give him a good shoe-beating."

The accused cried out :

" Your Worship, I never killed anybody before, and I will never kill anyone in future. Pardon me this time. I am a poor man and it will be a great favour to me."

But the chaprasis caught hold of him and began to carry out the Magistrate's orders to the very letter. The man was crying bitterly and when the shoe-beating was nearly finished, the Magistrate cried out :—

" Now, you *badmash* (wicked man), will you kill any person again ? "

" Never, never, Hazur," cried the culprit. " Never will I commit a murder as long as I live."

" *Khabardar* ! " (take care) said the Magistrate, " if you do it again I will send you to jail."

Then he made the man take an oath thrice not to kill anybody, and let him go.

When the accused had been released, the *Munshi* (clerk) submitted to the Magistrate the Sections of the *Indian Penal Code,* which provided capital punishment or transportation for life for the offence of murder.

" Oh ! the Penal Code ! " said the Magistrate, " that blessed book was written while I was away on leave in England."

AN UNFORTUNATE RESEMBLANCE

AN English nurse in India wanted donkey's milk for her little charge, and asked her servant to get a good healthy donkey for her inspection. She had a limited stock of Hindustani words at her disposal, and a distinction of masculine and feminine gender in her Indian vocabulary was out of the question. So she said :

" *Achchhá gadhá láo* " (good donkey bring).

The servant produced a good-looking donkey which, when left before the Nurse, stood stark still as the most disciplined soldier, looking very meek as if to recommend himself. But unfortunately he was not the thing the Nurse wanted. She was much upset at her servant's stupidity in bringing a male donkey for milking purposes. But she was at a loss to find a word in Hindustani for a female donkey. At last she said :

" This is a *Sáhib gadhá* (a gentleman ass). I want a *ma'm gadhá* " (lady ass)—and then pointing to herself—" like myself."

Poor Nurse ! She said 'gadhá' when she ought to have said 'gadhi.'

KALACHAND BABU'S ENGLISH

IN bygone days not much knowledge of English was required by candidates for even high posts in India. So Kalachand Babu with his smattering of English easily got a post on the staff of His Honour the Lieutenant-Governor of Bengal.

Once when he was conversing with His Honour he said:

"Sir, Sir, Your Honour lie, Sir."

As he came out of the room of the Governor the A.D.C. in attendance came and said to him:

"Kalachand, you have grossly insulted His Honour by saying 'Your Honour lies.' I fear he will take serious steps."

Kalachand Babu was not convinced, so he went to the Chief Secretary and asked:

"Sir, Sir, if gentleman speaking another gentleman tell—'Sir, Sir, you lie, Sir,' what then, Sir?"

"Oh," said the Chief Secretary, "I would whip the man who would say that to me."

Then Kalachand Babu went to the Under Secretary and asked:

"Sir, Sir, if a gentleman talking a gentleman talk 'Sir, Sir, you lie, Sir,' what then, Sir?"

"I would kick the man then and there," replied the Under Secretary.

Kalachand was now full of anxiety. He did

SOME TYPES OF INDIAN MEN.

sure to be realised after the lapse of a short period. I can wait for this short time, considering that I have waited so long."

Then the Raja called upon his daughter to explain what made her like the verses so much as to award such a precious gift as her diamond ring to the reciter.

The Princess replied :

"Father, I have grown so old and am not yet married. I had therefore made up my mind to run away to-night with the Prince to whom I was betrothed years ago. But the verses make me feel that if I could wait so long I can wait a little longer."

"Now," said the Raja, "it is the Mantriputra's (son of the Minister) turn to show cause why he struck his father."

"Sire," said the boy, "the Prince and the Princess have been well educated, so they could easily grasp the meaning of the Sanskrit verses ; but my father brought me up with so much indulgence that I neglected my education, and being unlettered I could not enjoy the beauty of the stanza. So in a fit of anger I struck my father on the face to punish him for not having brought me up strictly and carefully."

"Well," said the Raja, "this I can understand. But how do you account for your strange conduct, Mantriji (Sir Minister) ?"

"Prithwinath (Lord of the earth)," replied the Minister, "I considered myself lucky that my scapegrace boy, devoid of all education, only slapped me in the face, and did nothing more serious."

"A LITTLE KNOWLEDGE IS A DANGEROUS THING"

IN the early days of English rule in Bengal, there were not many Bengalis who could speak English. One of the villagers, Kanu Ram, picked up three words of English: "Yes," "No," and "Very well," and he would go on saying them day and night. Thus he acquired the reputation of being the master of the English language among his fellow-men.

One day an English magistrate came to the village, in which he lived, to hold an inquiry in a case of robbery with murder. Kanu Ram was presented to the magistrate by the villagers as their English-speaking mouthpiece.

The magistrate asked him, "Did you commit the robbery and murder at Rampur on Sunday night?"

"Yes," said Kanu Ram.

"Have you anything to say in your defence?"

"No," said Kanu Ram.

"Then you must be sentenced to death."

"Very well," said Kanu Ram.

Before Kanu Ram could grasp what had befallen him, he was pounced upon by constables and dragged away. Then he cried in his own language:

"What have I done to deserve this treatment?"

But his "Yes," "No," and "Very well" had sealed his doom, and it was too late for him to realise that "A little knowledge is a dangerous thing."

"A LITTLE KNOWLEDGE IS DANGEROUS"

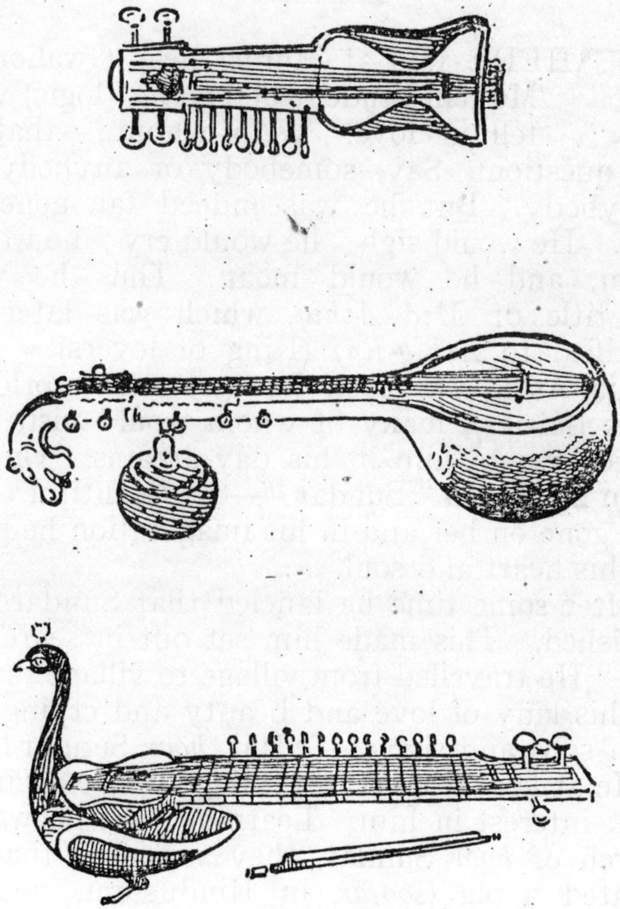

INDIAN MUSICAL INSTRUMENTS

MIA ASHIQ (Mr. LOVER)

THERE was at Murar, near Gwalior, a Moslem student of *montiq* (logic) who fell in love. With whom ?—that is the question. Say, somebody or anybody or everybody. But he was indeed far gone in love. He would sigh ; he would cry ; he would moon, and he would moan. Thus he won the title of *Miá Ashiq*, which was later on dignified to *Ashiq-Ráj* (King of lovers).

Miá Ashiq was soon known to the world of *hoors* (fairies), many of whom would visit and make love to him in his day-dreams. One of them he named " Sundar "—the Beautiful. He was gone on her and in his imagination he gave her his heart and soul.

After some time he fancied that Sundar had vanished. This made him set out in search of her. He travelled from village to village raving for his lady of love and beauty and crying out with sobs and sighs :—" Hái, *hoor* Sundar ! "

He at last arrived at a village where a family took interest in him. Learning that he was in search of *hoor* Sundar, they supposed that he wanted a pig (*soo-ar,* in Hindustani, mispronounced by the villagers of Central India and Rajputana as *hoor*). The pig, called Sundar, belonged to a neighbouring sweeper's family, and had lately run away. So they said to him :

" If you want to find *hoor* Sundar, we shall

MIÁ ASHIQ

shew you the place you can search successfully. But you must do one thing for us. We are hardly ever favoured by a learned Moslem's visit. You seem to be a man of learning, and as it is nightfall, can you not accept our hospitality for the night and read to us *Maulud sharif?* (religious sermons). Early in the morning one of us will lead you to yonder jungle where you are sure to find *hoor* Sundar if you search carefully. But will you kindly tell us why, being a Moslem, you are in quest of a *hoor?*"

"That is my affair," answered Miá Ashiq. "I am impatient to search the forest, but as I am half famished I thankfully accept your kind hospitality. I have no *Maulud sharif*, but I can read to you my book on *Montiq*, which I have got with me."

The ignorant villagers had never heard of *Montiq*, and thinking that it must be a great sacred subject, they sat around Miá Ashiq to hear it. They were very pleased to hear the Arabic text of *Montiq* read out to them, though they could not understand a word of it. Miá Ashiq was treated with respect to a rural repast and given a *charpai* (a bedstead having a bamboo or wooden frame with knitted straw-strings) to sleep on in the yard. Miá Ashiq did not have a wink of sleep, obsessed by thoughts of Sundar. So he got up at midnight, stole away from the house, and silently wended his way towards the forest where the people said he could find his sweetheart. He ranged the forest till daylight, regardless of all dangers, and crying out:

" Hai, *hoor* Sundar !
O, my Lailá, here is thy Majnu
O, my Shiri, here is thy Farád."*

He had not slept for two or three days and nights, and disappointment made him feel doubly fatigued. Sleep was weighing down his eyelids ; and being unable to walk any further he sank down and fell fast asleep. By chance the pig that had strayed away came to the spot, just when he was dreaming of Sundar and crying " Sundar," " Sundar," in his sleep. Being attracted by the name the pig came after him and began to lick his lips. Thinking that he was being kissed by the fairy Sundar, Miá Ashiq was enjoying an exquisitely thrilling sensation. Presently there came the sweeper, to whom the pig belonged, and set his dog upon the truant animal. The pig ran away, but the dog fell upon Miá Ashiq and took him by the nose. He roared with pain, which made the sweeper come to his rescue and separate the dog from him. Miá Ashiq was staggered to hear that such an unclean animal as a pig was licking his mouth, and the pain of his bleeding nose was too much to allow him to indulge in his love-dreams. Since then he ceased to have day-dreams of love-making in fairyland. Thus was cured a love-disease which the physicians gave up as incurable.

* Allude to the love-stories of " Lailá and Majnu " and " Shiri and Farad " in which the lovers searched for their sweethearts and were restored to them after great sufferings.

GAIN WITHOUT PAIN

THERE was a poor man who was very avaricious and wished to be rich in one day—and that without any energetic exertions. So he went to a magician and begged him hard for a charm with which he could invoke some spirit who would give him all he wanted. The magician at first tried to dissuade him, but finding him resolute he gave him a charm.

The man went home in high spirits and scarce delayed in putting the charm to use. Presently a gigantic giant appeared before him and thundered forth :—

"Order me, master, or I will kill you!"

The man shouted out :—

"Make me a palace fitted up with every object of comfort."

No sooner said than done. The palace was there with everything that the man could wish. The giant called for more work, failing which he would kill the man. The man ordered a pretty garden with flowers, evergreens, fountains, tanks, beautiful birds and beasts and all that he could name in one breath.

The order was carried out in the twinkling of an eye. Then the giant called for more orders with his usual threat.

The man was at his wits' end and muttered out :—

" For the present I have no orders to give. I will think of others to-morrow."

" Then I must kill you," said the giant in a terrific voice.

Fearing for his life, the man ran and ran till he came into the presence of the magician.

" What is the matter ? " asked the magician.

" LO, THE GIANT COMES TO KILL ME."

Gasping for breath the man cried out—" Save, oh save, my Lord—Lo ! the giant comes to kill me ! "

The giant, who had run after the man, was just going to fall upon him, but stopped short at the command of the magician.

" Hold," he said, " what do you want with this man ? "

" You know my rule," said the giant. " I will

work for a man so long as he gives me fresh orders, but I must kill him if he fails to do so."

"Well," said the magician, "you want work, I will give you work. There lies a dog with a crooked tail. Cut off the tail and make it straight."

The giant at once chopped it off, pulled it out straight, and hurled it on the ground. No sooner had he let it go than it became twisted again.

"No," said the magician, "you must make it straight and go on doing that till it is quite straight."

The giant stretched the tail straight, but every time he let it go it got twisted again. So that gave him an endless occupation.

"Now, my son," said the magician to the man, "go and live in peace, Your palace and garden have vanished. Never again seek wealth without due exertions. For such wealth is not free from the fear of a giant threatening to kill you. As for this dog's tail, it shows that our worldly affairs can never be straightened. They seem to be straight at times, but get twisted again."

THE MORAL OF MADNESS

THERE was a man who had a screw loose in his brain. He was well-to-do and had nothing to do to earn his bread. But he was busy, very busy, night and day. Early in the morning he used to go out and came back wet with perspiration for his noon-meal ; and he would go out again in the afternoon and return from his perspiring work late at night. People began to wonder what he did with himself all the while he was out of doors. On being asked, he simply said : "I am going to work." But nobody knew what the nature of the "work" was.

One day some men shadowed him and found that he went away to a distant field. He took off his dress and girded his loins and then began to carry big mounds of earth from one field to another and then back again. This he went on doing till he was streaming with perspiration. At intervals when he was tired out he was heard to say :—

"I cannot stand the strain of this work any longer ! How long have I to work like this ?"

The people who had shadowed him appeared and asked him the reason of his tiring himself with a useless work. The crazy man answered :

"Well, you people have gone mad and occupy yourselves with useless pursuits. You never help me and now come to taunt me with unmeaning questions."*

* This story is cited to show how we toil and moil in this life under a fancied responsibility, which is ascribed to Máyá (illusion). We are all mad in some sense and yet talk of others as mad.

THINGS ARE NOT WHAT THEY SEEM

MOURNINGS and marriages in India are really very grand affairs. For, in both, hundreds and thousands of people have to be fed, and many to be paid as well. The cost must be proportionate to a man's estate and often involves all that he has saved or can borrow. Many days before the last ceremony is over, relatives and friends have got to be invited to come and stay with the family; and they should be pleased to accept some presents when they leave.

In the case of a wedding, festivities extend over weeks. Gay decorations and influx of merry-making neighbours, friends, and relatives mark out the house where the happy event is to take place. Music, *nautch*, banquets and entertainments of all descriptions keep up the fever of excitement from day to day till the bride and bridegroom part after the nuptials. Even the poorest family signalises the approach of a marriage by some efforts at gaieties—the music being produced by at least one pipe and one drum.

Early one morning Lila, a little girl, who lived in a village in Bengal, woke up with the sound of such a pipe and a drum, and being inquisitive asked her mother :—

"Mother, mother, why have they started

playing the pipe and drum this morning at our house ?"

The mother replied : " Don't you know, my darling, you are going to be married to a nice boy your father has chosen for you, on Monday week ? To-day we put *haldi** on your body. The Astrologers say that this is the best day for it."

" Who is the nice boy, mother ? " asked Lila.

" He," said the mother, " is a handsome boy with fair complexion and comes from a good family. They are very well-to-do and all the girls of this village will envy your happiness."

" What is his name ? " asked the girl.

" Ramlal," replied the mother.

" Ramlal ? " said the girl, " there is no such handsome boy by the name of Ramlal in our village ! The only Ramlal I know of is a dark, ugly old man. I don't like him ! "

" You silly child ! " answered the mother, " how can you know a boy who lives at Decca, about a hundred miles from here ? "

" Hm ! " exclaimed the girl, and drew aside in a sulky mood.

The mother could not guess the cause of the girl's abrupt silence and tried to make her speak, but to no effect. The father came and then came other relatives ; and all of them entreated Lila to cheer up on the day of her luck and to speak out and tell the cause of her trouble.

* A yellow stuff with which the bride's body is rubbed and which is then washed off by a bath with ceremony. The custom differs in different parts of India.

At last the girl muttered out in sobs :—

" Mother married father, aunt married uncle, sister-in-law married brother—they all married at home, and in *my* case I am to be married to a boy of Decca or Calcutta, hundreds of miles away ! "

The girl's speech drew forth a hearty laugh from all that were present, but it was a hard task to make her understand that things were not as she fancied.

THE BLIND LEAD THE BLIND

THERE lived in a village four blind men, who had often heard an elephant talked of, and wondered greatly what it could possibly be like.

So, when one day an elephant was passing through the village, they begged of the rider to give them an opportunity of knowing it by touch. The rider allowed them to do so, and the four blind men were right glad to be led near to the animal, and to feel its stupendous body with their hands.

The elephant was soon on the move again, and one of the blind men began to talk of his sensational experience thus :—

"What a huge thing an elephant is! It is just like a pillar, or a thick round log."

"You are mistaken, my friend," said another blind man, "you must have felt a pillar and not an elephant. The elephant is like a thick rope with hair at the end."

"Both of you are deceived," said the third blind man. "You must surely have felt something else than an elephant, which is surely like a fan."

"My dear friends," said the fourth blind man, "all of you are quite wrong. How on earth could you feel an elephant if you describe it like that? It is neither a log, nor a rope, nor a fan, but a vast mass of flesh without shape or size, and without beginning or end."

"Yours is the most delusive idea," said the first blind man. "Never has a person described an elephant as being endless."

Thus they had a serious dispute among themselves. None would yield to the other.

A wise man was standing hard by, listening to the hot dispute with keen interest. When the disputants became wild with fury and came to blows, he approached them and begged them to be quiet.

"Hold, brothers," he exclaimed. "Do not quarrel but listen to me. You all are right and you all are wrong. When the first man says that the elephant is like a log, he means only the leg of the animal, the second man's rope represents its tail, the fan of the third man answers to its ear, and the fourth man is evidently describing its body. So you see you have had only the knowledge of *parts*, but you are disputing about the *whole*.

"Anyhow, you teach me a grand lesson: We are all blind in matters of religious truths, yet we would seek to lead others in realising the Grand Mysterious Being."

WHY WOMEN ARE VEILED IN INDIA

OR

A QUESTION OF JUSTICE

THERE reigned in a province Raja Gabboo Chand, whose Court was always famous for justice.

One day a house collapsed and killed some men. The owner of the house was summoned and sentenced to death. He pleaded :—

"What could I do, my lord? The masons did not take care to build the house strong, so it came down. It is not my fault."

Raja Gabboo Chand at once had the masons seized and ordered them to be beheaded. The masons pleaded :—

"It is not our fault, oh, you just king. It is the fault of the mortar-makers. The mortar was not strong enough."

The king let the masons go, but ordered the mortar-makers to be apprehended and put to death.

The mortar-makers appeared before him and pleaded :—

"Have mercy, upright king. The brick-makers are to blame and not we. They did not make the bricks strong enough."

The mortar-makers were released and the

brick-makers had to be executed in their stead. But they came and pleaded :—

"It was not our fault, O the justest of kings. The wood-cutters did not give us fuel enough to bake the bricks hard."

The wood-cutters had now to be punished, instead of the brick-makers. But they asked for pardon, saying :—

"Mercy, O incarnation of Justice! The fault is not ours. A party of your horsemen rode into our donkeys that were carrying the wood. Many of the donkeys threw off their loads and ran away. So there was a shortage of fuel."

The horsemen were to be punished ; but they came and pleaded :—

"What could we do? O the equal of God in justice! Some women were passing by and they looked at us and as we looked back at them we did not see the donkeys ahead. The result was as described by the wood-cutters."

So the women had to be punished. But as they could not be traced, a general punishment for all women was declared :—

"Henceforth no women shall look upon men. They must have veils over their faces."

THE AUTHORITY OF PRECEDENTS

PRECEDENTS are as binding on the Indian people in all their transactions* as on the Royal Courts of Justice in Fleet Street.

Once upon a time a fire broke out at the palace of a Raja. The question was: " Whose duty is it to extinguish the fire ? "

The Secretariat Officers were hurriedly summoned to look up the records for a precedent.

There had been no outbreak of fire at the palace within their memory. Consequently they had to send for one of the oldest officials. This gentleman, on arriving, directed them to seek for a precedent in the records, fifty years old.

The fire was spreading all the time while the officers were busy unearthing the records, fifty years old.

Before they were successful in their hunt for the required precedent, their office caught fire and they had to escape.

Eventually the palace was burnt down, but the question of precedent remained unsolved.

II.

When a party of Oders (Non-Aryan diggers) was encamped near the city of Hyderabad, I

* All the chiefs and even petty Zemindars keep records which are consulted on each recurrence of a similar case.

was extremely pained to see how cruelly they killed their pigs.

I saw the head-man and asked him :—" Why don't you kill your pigs at a stroke instead of

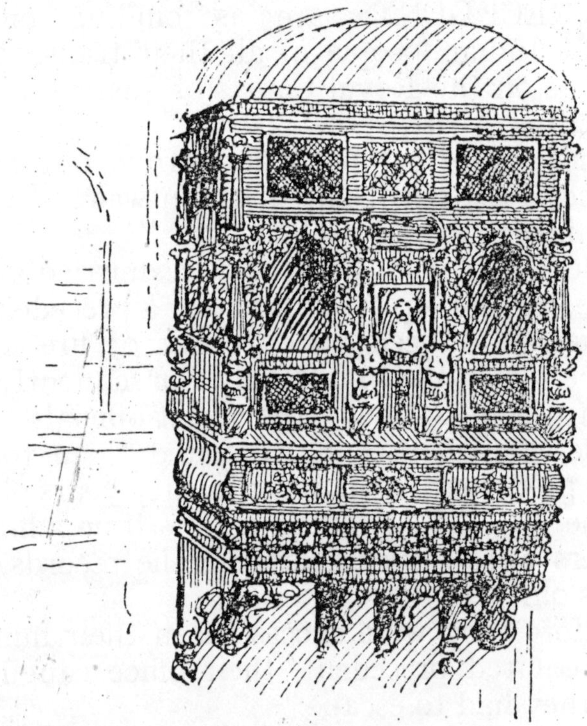

THE BALCONY OF A HOUSE.

first setting a dog on them and then piercing them through and through with spears ? "

" Well, Sir," answered the man, " there is no precedent for what you say. We cannot depart from the way of our ancestors."

Such is the force of Precedent and Customs and the blind reverence paid to them !

POLITENESS CARRIED TO EXCESS

TWO gentlemen, scions of the Royal family of Lucknow, were waiting for a train on the platform of a railway station. As the train arrived, the station-master opened the door of a compartment for them to enter. But instead of entering, one of the gentlemen said with a sweeping bow to the other ;—

" After you, sir."

The other, bending doubly low, said :—

" Sir, I am your slave in attendance and hence must follow."

The first gentleman promptly replied :—

" Sir, it is I that am the slave. So sir takes precedence and I follow."

The second gentleman : " How can that be possible ? Sir comes first and I after."

This *après vous* business was going on without any indication of terminating when the train started and left behind the over-polite gentlemen to settle the question which of them was to have the honour of entering the train first. They, however, passed strong remarks on the conduct of the engine-driver and the guard, who lacked politeness to such an extent as to have omitted to say :—

" After you, sirs."

People of India are now gradually realising that :—

" Time and trains wait for no man."

A QUESTION OF BIRTH

MANY years ago there was an old blind man who sought the service of a Raja. He gave out that he was an expert in testing jewels, domestic animals and persons. The Raja employed him on a small pittance.

It was not long before the old man was called upon to test some pearls, and afterwards some diamonds, and lastly a horse. On each of these occasions the Raja was on the point of paying the exorbitant sum charged by the merchants. But the old man pointed out in each case some real defect and thus did the Raja a great service by saving his money. The Raja was so much pleased with the old man that he gave him some copper coins in reward.

One day when the old man was alone in the Raja's presence he said very modestly :—

"Your Highness, will you forgive me if I tell you an unpleasant truth ?"

"Yes," said the Raja, "you may say anything without fear of incurring my displeasure."

"Then," said the old blind man, lowering his voice to a whisper, "will you care to learn that you are not the son of a Raja ?"

"How dare you ?" said the Raja angrily.

"Pardon me," said the old man, "you promised not to be angry."

The Raja : "You must prove your words, or I will cut off your head."

The old man : "If you want proof, do as I say. Go into the Palace, and drop down pretending heart-disease. You should writhe and toss as if you were going to die. Never seem to get better when the physicians administer to you any medicine. Let me be summoned to attend you last of all."

The Raja acted up to these instructions faithfully till at last the old man was called to attend him. He at first examined the pulse of the Raja and then said feigning despair :—

"The disease is fatal and the Raja is going to die in about an hour. The only remedy in such a case as this is the blessing of one's father."

No sooner had this been said than the Raja uttered a piteous cry and said :—"Oh ! then I am doomed, for my father died long ago. How can he come and bless me ? Farewell to you all, my life is done."

The Mother Rani who had heard all this from behind a screen, could no longer contain herself. She at once ordered her maids to ask all the people to leave her son's room. This having been done, she rushed into the room and said in haste to the Raja :—"My son, don't despair of recovery. I have just sent for your father to come and bless you."

"Mother, Mother," said the Raja, "what do you mean ? How can you get my father, who is in Heaven, to come and bless me ? You must tell me before I allow you to bring him."

"Then," replied the Mother Rani, "you

must be told the truth. You are not the son of the late Raja. When I gave birth to a dead child I was so anxious to conceal the fact that I asked my maids to smuggle in any new-born child, imposing on them the strictest secrecy. By chance a child was born to a Mahajan (money-lending Baniya) that very night, and it was brought to me in exchange for a large sum of money—and you are that child. The *Baniya*, though very old, is still living, and I will——"

"Enough," interrupted the Raja, "I am all right now and I don't need his blessing."

Saying this he went to his outer chamber and ordered the old blind man to be called in. When he entered, the Raja demanded :—

"How could you know the fact of my birth ?"

The old man said respectfully :—

"I knew the pearls by their smell,
I knew the diamonds by the touch,
I knew the horse by screwing its ears, and
I knew that you are the son of a *Baniya** by
your generosity."

* Usurer.

A MATTER OF CONSCIENCE

THERE was a man in Calcutta who was very lazy. He had no go in him and would not exert himself to better his circumstances. He looked to divine help for a happy turn of fortune. So he used to go to the temple of the goddess Káli* and pray to her to send him some good luck. One day he prostrated himself before Káli and beat his head on the ground, praying repeatedly:

"O Mother Káli, Mother Káli, let me have one hundred rupees. I will sacrifice to thee a pair of buffaloes."

On the next day the man by chance made a profit of one hundred rupees in a transaction. This he fancied to be the answer to his prayer. But the thought of sacrificing a pair of buffaloes weighed on his mind as a nightmare; for he was loath to part with a *cowri*† of his gain. So he went one day to the temple and prayed hard to Káli to let him off with one buffalo. He came away with the idea that his prayer was granted. But he was so unwilling to pay the price of even one buffalo that he went to the temple again and petitioned the goddess to grant the sub-

* At Kalighat, southern part of the city. 'Calcutta' is derived from '*Kalighata.*'

† A shell used as money of the least value.

stitution of a pair of goats for a buffalo. After some time he found out that even this was too much for him. Yet again he went to the temple and prayed for the acceptance of one goat instead of two. This too proved to be beyond his power in the course of time ; but the thought of his being indebted to Káli for the sacrifice of a goat, gave his conscience no rest. At last he went to the temple again and after repeated prostrations with his head rolling on the ground, he prayed :—

"Protection ! O, Mother Káli, Thou knowest the poverty of thy son. If thou dost not, who else would ? A son is always offending, but a mother is always forgiving. So forgive, forgive, O mother, thy unworthy son who has no refuge but thee. If thou hast excused me thus far, why wilt not thou remit me the sacrifice of a goat ? Please do release me from the vow altogether by excusing the goat. Thou wilt not surely die of hunger. If thou art badly in need of eating a sacrifice, I offer thee all the insects that fly by thy head. Please do catch the flies and mosquitoes and eat them, bestowing on me the merit of the sacrifice. I do hope thou will content thyself with the flies and not look for the goat from me." (Supposing that his prayer had appealed to the Káli successfully, he continued) : "That is like a real good forgiving Mother. No god or goddess is greater than thee, O my Mother Káli. Art thou sure thou art contented and ready to grant me more favours ? Thou knowest, mother, 'much always wants more' ; then why not my little ? So if thou hast given me a hundred, thou must give me a thousand. Now, give me a thousand rupees and test my vow. I will never fail to give you two buffaloes in sacrifice this time. If thou hast no faith in my vow, thou hadst better deduct the price of the buffaloes and send me down the balance only."

A MATTER OF FANCY
(A True Ghost Story)

THERE lived in the village of Kaliá* (Jessore, Bengal) a gentleman named Tarachand Harchowdhuri. He was returning alone from a feast at the dead of night. His way lay across a big lonely field in the middle of which stood a solitary tree,† accredited with many ghostly traditions. Undaunted he was passing the tree when all of a sudden a branch moved and made a rustling noise. There was no wind to stir it nor any visible cause. Naturally he took fright and ran towards the nearest house which happened to belong to one of his own tenants. On arriving there he fell senseless at

* A centre of the intelligent Vaidyas. This small village now claims about 200 graduates.

† Called *sardá gách*, which is a favourite home for nightly ghosts. These ghosts were believed to hold courts after midnight and vanish at day-dawn. Sometimes a man might fall in with the ghosts, who, if they kindly spared his life, allowed him to take part in the feasts and gave him sweetmeats to eat. In the morning he would wake up to find that he was lying on the grass with some dead insects or locusts by him, which were served to him by the ghosts as sweetmeats. An *ojhá* (exorcist) lived near the village, who, it is said, had many ghosts in his employ. He employed the ghosts in many ways, one of which was to carry him in his palanquin. Once upon a time the ghosts were carrying him over a marshy land of paddy-crop (the rice and jute plants of Bengal flourish in the water of the boggy lands). Their approach scared some birds which flew away suddenly making some noise, at which the exorcist gave a start. The ghosts at once took the opportunity of doing their master to death, for he had betrayed fear, and to be frightened always spells fatal results to an exorcist.

the door and when brought round he explained the cause of his fright. His tenant, Mrityunjay Dháli, took up a long bamboo club and came out to escort him home. When they had approached near his house he stopped short and whispered to his follower :—

" Look there, Mrityunjay, there is a burglar lurking near the wall to break into my house."

The tenant also spied the object of his remark and made a dash towards it with his raised club. Down came the club on a plank with a crashing din and smashed some of the earthen pots that were under it. Both of them wondered how they could be deluded like that and they retired to the place whence they had observed the supposed thief, to test their sight again. On closer observation they could make out that the moon-beams coming through the branches of a spreading tree cast a shadow having the appearance of a man.

This made the gentleman think that there was a possibility of his senses being likewise deceived in the previous case ; and he was eager to ascertain whether it was a real ghost that shook the tree or merely his imagination. So, accompanied by a party of men, armed with clubs, he went back to the solitary tree, the supposed home of a malicious ghost, and as such dreaded by all people at night. As soon as the party went near the tree the branches shook and the leaves rustled. With the cry : " Victory to Ram "* they attacked the branches

* The name of " Ram " (God or Vishnu's incarnation) is supposed to scare away malicious ghosts.

with their clubs, which, to their astonishment, brought down a shower of rats. They could now easily guess the cause of the frightening activities of the tree and the source of all the traditions associated with it. On a search they found out that innumerable rats inhabited the tree, living in the holes during the daytime and coming out at night to eat the sacrifices offered to the supposed ghost at twilight. Late at night they ran about on the branches and held their merry sports, undisturbed by human interference. The noise of a man's approach made them fly from the branches towards the holes in the trunk of the tree, and that accounted for the phenomenon which had been till then ascribed to some ghosts' agency.

A QUESTION OF PARTY-FEELING

IN India debates are often held between parties holding different opinions. Such debates are called *shástrárthas* ; and it is very interesting to watch the Pandits engaged in exciting discussions.

Years ago a serious debate was arranged between two parties at Benares. The point at issue was whether some reforms should be carried out in social customs based on religion. The parties were arrayed against each other, both confident of winning the day.

Now, when the mouthpiece of one party got up to speak, the members of the other party stopped their ears and turned their faces when the speaker was loudly cheered and applauded by his own party. It was *vice versa* when the leader of the Opposition began his speech. By chance one of the first party had his ears not quite closed. So he caught a phrase used by the speaker, which was not grammatically correct. He at once howled out :—

" Down with him, he doesn't know grammar !"

The cry was taken up by the rest of his party and then began a hot contest as to the phrase being right or wrong grammatically. All voices joined in citing rules from Sanskrit grammar, till at last the tumult was so great that the debate had to be closed by the Maharaja who was presiding over it.

On parting, members of both sides were overheard to say that their adversary leader's speech contained not a single scrap of argument which they could consider convincing. Of course, they were very good judges, for they had listened to each other with closed ears.

not know what to do to propitiate his Master. He prayed the whole night and gave *pujah* (offerings) to all the stars that influence destiny.

Early in the morning he put on his forehead some charmed stuff that was believed to propitiate offended persons and went his way to Belvedere (Residence of the Lieut.-Governor in Calcutta) with some presents for His Honour.

Quivering like a goat under a butcher's knife, he first saw the Head Jamadar (usherer) to ascertain if he had any unpleasant orders against himself and then knocked with a faltering hand at the door of the Lieutenant-Governor's sitting room.

"Who is it?" asked the Lieutenant-Governor.

"Your Humble—My Lord, Sir," answered Kalachand with a faint and quivering voice.

Lieutenant-Governor: "Oh, Kala Babu, come in. What do you want?"

Kalachand: "Nothing, Sir, My Lord. Your humble brought some *magnoes** for Your Honour, Sir."

Lieutenant-Governor: "But you look very run down. What's the matter with you?"

Kalachand: "Nothing, My Lord, Sir, Your Honour — Your humble has Benaresing †—whole night benaresing—benaresing, no little eye-shutting (sleep), Sir."

Lieutenant-Governor: "How could you go to Benares and return in a night, Kala Babu?"

Kalachand: "No going Benares, Sir. Throat,

* Mangoes.

† Benares is called Kashi by all Hindus, and *Kashi* in Bengal means *cough*. So Kala Babu translated coughing with the word 'Benaresing.'

Sir,—here Sir—impatient Sir, whole night Sir."

Lieutenant-Governor: "Oh, you had a sore throat. You must go to a Doctor."

Kalachand: "Sir, Sir—I will eat you, Sir!"

Lieutenant-Governor: "Hello! eat me? What do you mean, Kalachand? How will you digest me?"

Kalachand: "No, Sir. I will give you a eating, Sir. Your humble's daughter, Sir—Marriage, Sir—I must eat* you, Sir."

Lieutenant-Governor: "How old is your daughter?"

Kalachand: "Half-past twelve years, Sir, Your Honour."

Lieutenant-Governor: "Half-past twelve? You mean twelve years and a half. Your daughter is too young for marriage."

Kalachand: "No, Sir—You *lie*—No, no—You fault, Sir—Half-past twelve too larger for marry, Sir—You must come for eating, Sir—Your Honour."

Lieutenant-Governor: "When is the dinner?"

Kalachand: "Quarter gone night, Sir—twenty date going† January."

Lieutenant-Governor: "All right—Kala Babu, I will come."

Kala Babu made about twenty salaams and left the room the happiest of men—though he entered it as the most miserable of beings.

* Feed.

† Current.

"HAZUR'S PANKHA"

THERE was a settlement-officer in the province of the Punjab who was very kind-hearted and sympathetic. He knew Hindustani pretty well and could speak it with ease, so he did not depend on his Munshis (clerks) but always tried to get first-hand information from the ryots (tenants), and to right any injustice done to any of them.

He held his office in his Bungalow, and made it a rule that all who wanted to have justice should assemble on the verandah and make their application personally one by one. He did not allow any of his *chaprasis* to wait on the verandah to intercept petitioners not willing to pay them tips; but the Pankha-puller* had to be there, for without him the officer's room would have been too hot for anything.

One day when he called a petitioner in, the punkha suddenly stood still.

"*Pankha-khincho*" (pull the punkha), cried out the officer.

* Any officer in India not privileged to get away to the hills in the hot months must have a *pankha* and a pankha-puller to keep his office cool. The pankha is hung right over the officer's seat, and ropes are passed through a hole in the walls to join the pankha, and the pankha-puller who sits on the verandah as a miserable specimen of mankind pulling away at the pankha and dozing at the same time, or pulling and dozing by turn.

SOME TYPES OF INDIAN MEN.

No response.

" Pankha-khincho ! " again ; still no response. The officer got very angry and cried :

" What the deuce is the matter with the *pankha-wala* ? "

The man who had come in with his petition said :

" Hazur, I am the last petitioner and there is nobody left on the verandah to pull the pankha. If Hazur orders I will go and pull it till some other petitioner turns up."

" What do you mean ? " asked the officer, " where is my pankha-puller ? "

" We do not know if Hazur keeps any," replied the ryot. " It is the petitioner whom I have ever seen pulling Hazur's pankha. I took it up from the man who just left Hazur's office."

The officer on inquiry learnt that the *Pankha-wala* had issued an order that anybody, who came to petition the *sahib*, would each in turn have to pull his pankha. The officer then arranged that no petitioner should wait on the verandah but should drop their *arjis* (petitions) in a letter-box which he placed there. He had the key of the box himself and would attend to the complaints personally, on the spot, *i.e.*, the ryot's fields, at some fixed hour in the morning.

Now the *pankhawala* was at first dismayed, but he soon contrived a method of righting things. He seated himself comfortably on the petition-box and when any man came with an *árji,** he would not move to allow the latter to drop it in the box unless he was paid a tip or relieved of the pankha-pulling work.

Another day the pankha suddenly came to a standstill. It would not move in spite of the officer's repeated orders of " *Pankha Khincho.*"

The officer came out to the verandah, and seeing nobody, cried at the top of his voice :—

" Pankhawala ! "

The ryot who had been pulling the *pankha* and had not gone far away, came rushing back and making many salaams, said :

" Hazur, pardon me. My cattle will die if I do not go and attend to them immediately."

The officer replied :

" But who prevents you from going ? "

" Hazur's *pankha !* " said the ryot. " The *pankha-Kash* (pankha puller) gave strict orders that I should not move till another petitioner arrived."

" But what did you come here for ? " asked the officer.

Ryot : " I came to leave a petition, Hazur."

Officer : " Then why did you not leave it and go away without listening to the *pankha-wala ?*"

Ryot : " How could I leave it, Hazur ? The man sat on the petition-box stopping the hole, and not moving till I agreed to his terms. Besides, how could I make a scene on Hazur's verandah and refuse to pull *Hazur's pankha ?* "

* Petition.